THE ZAMBEZI

THE ZAMBEZI

River of the Gods

Jan and Fiona Teede

ANDRE DEUTSCH

First published 1990 by
Andre Deutsch Limited
105-106 Great Russell Street, London WC1B 3LJ

Text and photographs © 1990 Jan & Fiona Teede
Illustrations © 1990 Larry Norton
Design by Caroline Calascione

British Library Cataloguing in Publication Data
Teede, Jan
    The Zambezi : a photographic journey.
    1. Africa. Countryside adjacent to Zambezi river.
Description & travel
    I. Title II. Teede, Fiona
916.79

ISBN 0-233-98592-1

Printed in Singapore

for Leo and Sheila Teede

ACKNOWLEDGMENTS

We should like to thank the following for their invaluable
support in the production of this book. Larry Norton and
Caroline Calascione for their outstanding artwork and
design, and Nina Fircks for her enthusiasm on the
publishing side. All are, coincidentally, Zimbabweans.
In the field we are indebted to Paul and Eunice Fisher and
Paul Logan, for their help and hospitality in Zambia, the
department of National Parks and Wildlife Management in
Zimbabwe, Richard Calder, for his skilled piloting in
Mozambique, and Patrick van der Muelen for his assistance
at Cabora Bassa. Many others have been a source of help
and encouragement. We thank them all.

CONTENTS

LIST OF ILLUSTRATIONS

AFRICA

ZAIRE

ZAMBIA

MALAWI

ZAMBEZI

ZIMBABWE

MOZAMBIQUE

BOTSWANA

MADAGASCAR

INTRODUCTION

For us the Zambezi has been a holiday retreat for most of our lives. After only a five hour journey from home, we could experience an extravaganza of bird and animal life in a wilderness seemingly forgotten in the race for development. The draw of such natural splendour is so powerful that it is difficult to return to the bonds of an urban existence. We hope the same may be true for our grandchildren, and that unlike much of the world's natural heritage, this area does not become merely a faint memory and historical record.

In 1985 we decided to take the plunge and become full time natural history photographers. The Zambezi provided the obvious subject for a long term project. The Rhodesian war had curtailed access to the river from the early 1970s until the end of hostilities in 1980, so a major pictorial study had not been undertaken before. The Zimbabwean part of the river presented no major problems. In Zambia travel often involved cutting our way through the bush and the authorities were nervous about our photographing anything, including waterfalls. The short section in Angola had to be very curtailed owing to the guerilla war there. On arrival at one border post we had to fill in endless exit formalities, although there was no road on the other side. Mozambique is still in the grip of a bloody internicine war, and it was this part that presented the most obstacles. A chance meeting with an engineer allowed us access to the Cabora Bassa wall, but the photographs had to be taken from the mountains out of sight of the Frelimo guard. Only later did we discover that these hills were extensively mined. The rest of the lower river was done in a series of 'hit and run' raids when the security situation allowed.

The Zambezi is 2700 kilometres from source to mouth, the fourth longest river in Africa after the Nile, the Congo and the Niger. First the Arabs, then the Portuguese and finally David Livingstone tried to use it as a trade route to the interior.

Vasco da Gama moored at the mouth in 1498 on his way to the East Indies. He christened it *Rios dos bons sinais*, the river of good omens, in the hope that it would become a lucrative passage for the gold trade. It was not until David Livingstone, however, that the river was explored in its entirety. The Zambezi became an obsession for the Scottish doctor, the foundation of his dreams and the inspiration of his life's work. On an epic journey between 1853 and 1856 he followed the course of the river from its upper reaches to the sea. He brought the Victoria Falls to the attention o the world, described numerous

species of unknown plant and animal life and filled in great gaps on the map of Africa. It was a monumental feat of endurance. Two years later he returned to the river with a steamboat. The expedition was halted by the impassable Cabora Bassa rapids, an area he had avoided on his great walk two years previously. Livingstone's plan to use the Zambezi as 'God's highway' to the interior was finally thwarted.

As the colonizers lost interest so the river was left to the native peoples. Much of its course from north western Zambia to the Indian Ocean in Mozambique remains sparsely inhabited and large tracts provide an unspoilt refuge for wildlife. It is an untamed river, a fragile and complex ecosystem. No doubt the lack of human settlement and development along its banks owes much to the disease-carrying tsetse fly and the anopheles mosquito — small things can have far reaching effects.

But times are changing. The burgeoning population of the region has fuelled a demand for more land in marginal areas and the wildlife reserves are being encroached upon by human settlement. At present the Zambezi is the only river of its size which has little commercial importance beyond the production of power. That may change. There are plans to divert its waters for irrigation and to build more dams, one of which would flood the unique middle Zambezi Valley. Geologists are searching its bed for oil and minerals. The tsetse fly, Africa's most effective game ranger, is being gradually eradicated. Poachers are destroying the wildlife, notably the black rhino. Not long ago the Zambezi valley boasted the largest population of this species in the world. Now few remain.

We do not pretend to know all the answers and dare not venture too much into the future. But perhaps this book will convey, in some measure, an impression of what this unique wilderness is today, and why it should be preserved.

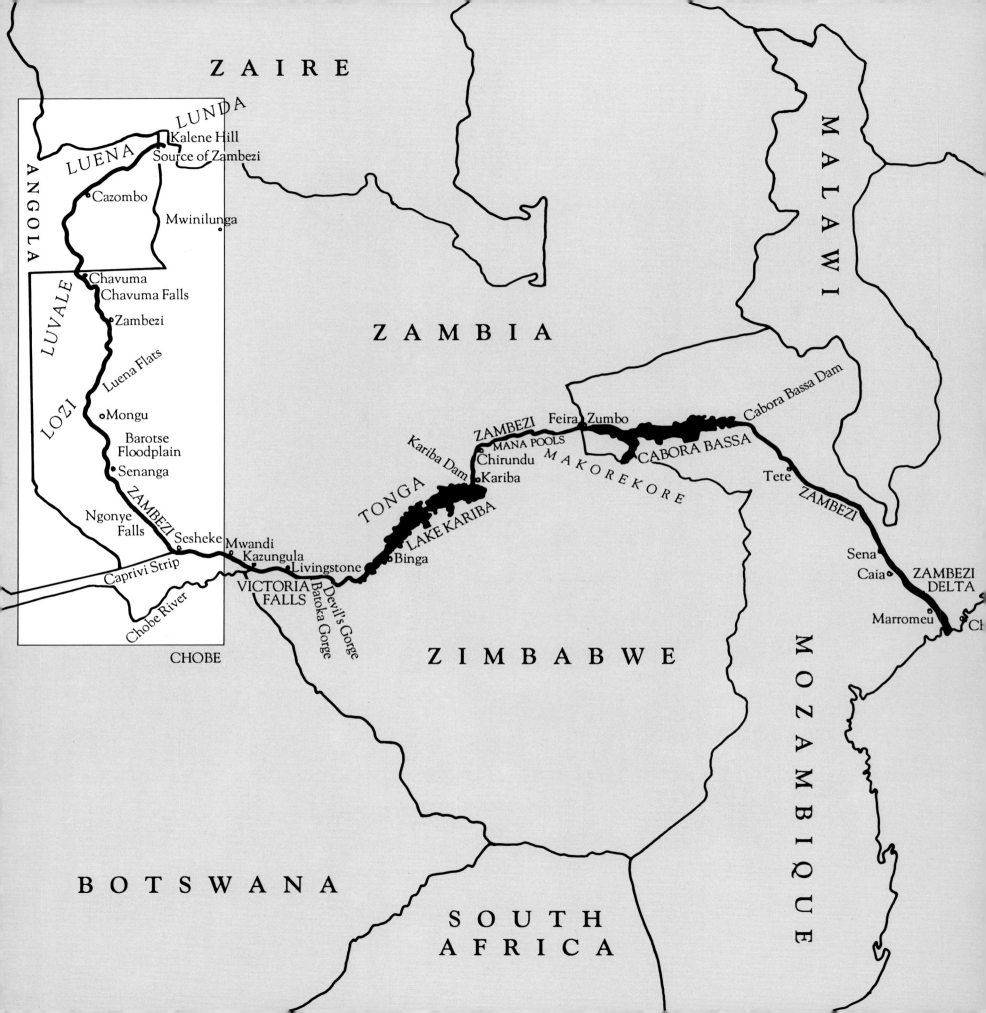

ZAIRE

LUNDA

LUENA

Kalene Hill
Source of Zambezi

ANGOLA

Cazombo

Mwinilunga

LUVALE

Chavuma

Chavuma Falls

Zambezi

Luena Flats

LOZI

Mongu

Barotse
Floodplain

Senanga

ZAMBEZI

Ngonye
Falls

Sesheke

Mwandi

Kazungula

Livingstone

Caprivi Strip

Chobe River

CHOBE

ZAMBIA

MALAWI

Kariba Dam

TONGA

Lake Kariba

Binga

ZAMBEZI

MANA POOLS

Chirundu

Kariba

MAKOREKORE

Feira Zumbo

CABORA BASSA

Cabora Bassa Dam

Tete

ZAMBEZI

Sena

Caia

ZAMBEZI
DELTA

Marromeu

Ch

VICTORIA
FALLS

Batoka Gorge

Devil's Gorge

ZIMBABWE

MOZAMBIQUE

BOTSWANA

SOUTH
AFRICA

UPPER ZAMBEZI

With mounting excitement we strode along the track towards our goal. The forest closed in around us and huge spiders' webs clung to the trees, their landlords suspended motionless, waiting to pounce. Blue duiker spoor zigzagged across our path. The silence was oppressive.

About five kilometres north of the Zambezi source, in the Katanga Province of Zaire, are the headwaters of the Congo river. The Luakwa hills, rising to an altitude of some 1500 metres, form the backbone of this central part of the Southern African Plateau. They create the barely perceptible divide between these two great rivers, the Congo and the Zambezi.

We were following in the footsteps of Frank Stanley Arnott, a missionary who first discovered and mapped the headwaters of the river in 1886. As we clambered downwards between the trees, avoiding a python lying cold in the shadows, clouds of mosquitoes swarmed around our ears. We heard the trickle of a stream and pushed our way towards it. At last, flowing between a maze of moss-covered tree roots, were the sparkling waters of a tiny Zambezi. Brilliantly coloured butterflies flitted silently between the twisted lianas. They would rest momentarily on a leaf, bathed in a shaft of sunlight and, just as we crept forward to snatch a photograph, would slip elusively out of reach.

We followed the stream, listening for it as it disappeared underground, and traced it back as far as we could, to the point where it oozed out of the black quagmire. Finally we had reached our goal, the fountain-head of the river. The slow struggle through 'the sloppy country', as Arnott described the marshland beween the Zambezi and Congo rivers, was now forgotten.

The Lunda people

Leaving the source, we drove to Ikelenge, the small village centre of the area. Rolling grasslands, punctuated by belts of Brachystegia woodland and modelled by the channels of numerous small streams, stretched out on either side of us. Searching for a place to camp, we were astounded to find ourselves on a track through a large dairy and beef farm. This estate, on a rocky outcrop known as Kalene Hill, is owned by the Fishers, descendants of Dr and Mrs Walter Fisher, who started the first mission in the region in 1906.

Legend has it that a chief living nearby wanted to move south. It was the rainy season and, finding his passage blocked by the extensive marshlands, he dug up a variety of magic roots. These he boiled, dried and crushed. As he walked, he threw handfuls of the 'nsompu' dust ahead of him, moaning incantations to the spirits. Each time the offerings settled, a hill appeared, and using these as stepping stones, he was able to cross the mire. Kalene Hill marks the beginning of this sandstone ridge.

From the top of the hill we looked over the undulating, wooded plains of Zambia, Zaire and Angola. Mist rose from the river valleys and we could trace the path of the Zambezi below. Dr Fisher had stood here, searching for tell-tale ribbons of smoke from villages deep in the forests, where the Lunda people hid in terror from Ovimbundu, Luena and Chokwe slave-raiders. Using the smoke as a guide, the missionary had taken medical aid and the Christian message to the distrustful natives. The curious people had watched the scalpel work its magic and believed injections were the answer to all ills. There was great rivalry among the patients and a medical operation was considered a much-coveted privilege. The news of the gentle white man spread and the Lunda came to settle within reach of the safety of the hospital. The mission was moved nearer permanent water and little remains of the old site except crumbling walls and the graves of the doctor and his wife.

In spite of the influx of refugees from Zaire and Angola, the Lunda, an offshoot from the Mwantiyanvwa empire in Zaire, remain the dominant tribe in the region. These peaceful people moved south to escape from the slave-traders and relied on hunting for their survival. The increasing population and ignorance of conservation has resulted in the elimination of most of the wildlife in the area. Even the small birds have suffered, decimated by the continuous use of birdlime. As hunting is no longer viable, the Lunda have turned to subsistence farming and fishing. They grow millet, cassava, groundnuts, beans and a variety of fruit, including the most delicious pineapples. Pigs, goats and chickens scuttle between the untidy villages, shepherded by a string of scantily clad, pot-bellied children. The men spend the day in idle conversation with their friends while the women work. They plough, plant and harvest, hew wood and prepare food. Some fish with rectangular baskets, trawling in the shallows after a few fingerlings, while others use conical, baited fish traps.

Meandering through Angola

As it continues along its course, the river swells rapidly, fed by numerous tributaries and continuous underground seepage. Eighty kilometres from the source, it winds its way into Angola, cutting through the grey sand plains of the undeveloped Angolan province of Molwezi. The population is sparse and is congregated along the river. Windblown soils and low rainfall make agriculture difficult, and the Luena or Lovale villagers are reliant on fishing. Today, severely affected by the war, many have left their homes and fled to safety in Zambia.

The Zambezi's numerous tributaries dry up during the winter months. The rains begin again in October. By late November the feeder streams are full. It is time for the spawning run of the mud barbel. The Lovale build fences of reeds across the shallow channels, leaving

a narrow gap behind which a semicircular trap is constructed. The barbel swim through the hole as they move upstream and are caught and speared.

'We can't club them,' a fisherman told us. 'The other fish will hear the skulls cracking and turn back.'

Kazombo is the only major settlement. Built on a granite promontory 30 metres above the river, the village was founded as a mission station by Dr Fisher in 1899, before he moved to Kalene. On several occasions slavers stole his boat at night to ferry their human cargo across the river. He chained it to an iron stake, but the thefts continued.

'Today I had to sink the boat. We are more cut off than ever, but we cannot be party to this cruelty,' he wrote.

Chavuma town

The river gradually swings southward, re-entering Zambia and doubling in width as the steep banks fall away. A few kilometres downstream from the border lies the small town of Chavuma, which has grown up around a mission station and is situated on a hill overlooking the Zambezi and the Kashiji Plains beyond. Up to 15 years ago these plains were covered with teeming herds of wildebeeste and lechwe antelope during the rains, but uncontrolled hunting has left the grasslands barren.

'There was no road here until the 1940s,' said missionary Paul Logan, who was born here. 'I can remember my father going on a shopping trip to Livingstone once a year. It would take him four weeks to get there by barge, and eight weeks to get back.'

Below the town the river is forced through a small gap in an outcrop of hard volcanic rock and tumbles over a three metre-high waterfall. The water sounds as if it is being blown through a hole, 'Chaa-VUM-aah', hence the name of the cataract and the village. Just below this, boatmen in canoes often so laden that water laps over the sides, manage to paddle their dugouts deftly across the powerful current without mishap. The aid-sponsored ferry is rather less reliable!

We camped on a long sandbank, from where we could launch our inflatable dinghy, the *Chikwekwe*, and bathe in safety away from the few remaining crocodiles. While we were there, a young man of the Lunda tribe contrasted the lives of the two peoples:

'We are Lunda. We live this side of the river so we can hunt in the forests, and collect honey.' He pointed across the water and continued, 'They are Luena, fishermen. If you visit the Kashiji river you can find their nets.'

Once, a long time ago, Nyambe made the world and made Kamunu, the first man.

Kamunu made a spear and killed a lechwe ram and ate it.

'Oh man, you have fallen into evil. Why have you killed this animal, your kin? You must not eat him. You are all my children,' cried Nyambe, and drove him away.

After a year Nyambe allowed Kamunu to return and gave him a garden. He was allowed to kill and eat the buffalo, eland and elephant that came to destroy his crops, but each time Nyambe would take something in return. Then Nyambe left the earth. He sent his daughter to us and she bore the Lozi nation.'

As we talked, an ancient crone beat cassava in a mortar. Her cheeks were scarified, the insignia of beauty and womanhood. She grinned at us and we saw that her incisors had been filed into sharp points. We wanted a photograph but she fled into one of the huts. These tribal practices have been banned by the government and only a few old people bear the scars of initiation.

Interspersed with these two tribes are the innovative Chokwe, slave-raiders of old from Angola. They are born traders, dealing in food, clothing and anything that can be bought and sold. Their commodities have changed, but they have not forgotten the lessons of their Portuguese masters.

Most of the villages consist of square mud houses, with steeply pitched, thatched roofs and verandahs. Grass fires are burnt indoors and the escaping smoke preserves the structural timbers from insect damage. Many charred remains are seen as testimony to this often catastrophic custom.

From Chavuma the river flows south between steep, forested banks, broken by small tributaries every 10 – 15 kilometres. The waters are deep and calm, the landscape monotonous. The abandoned caperings of two young clawless otters provided a welcome diversion early one morning.

Wooden dug-outs cruise between the scattered villages. At the main centres, Zambezi (originally known as Balovale) and Chitokiloki, a mission station further downstream, the river margins bear the scars of deforestation and erosion. Every year, clearing for agriculture, debarking for making ropes, blankets and coarse cloth, and uncontrolled bush-fires further damage the environment.

The Nyamboma rapids near the Kabompo – Zambezi confluence mark the beginning of the Barotse floodplain. This vast prairie covers some 8000 square kilometres, through which a limpid Zambezi wends its way, sending out numerous branches over the grey-white sands.

The kingdom of the Lozi

It was nearing the end of March. We pushed on to Mongu, the commercial centre of Barotseland, in order to be in time for the famous Lozi Kuomboka ceremony. The Lozi kingdom extends from Lukulu in the north to Senanga in the south, and from the Kwando river in the west to the Kafue river in the east.

The Lozi originated in the southern region of the Congo and may be related to the Lunda. They are ruled by the *litunga* (king), who governs from the northern capital of the region, Lealui. A second capital at Nalolo, 50 kilometres downstream, was built to control the southern half of the kingdom and is presided over by the chief princess, *litunga-la-mboela*.

The Lozi are tall and well-built. Although gifted and friendly, they have two major faults: they are compulsive liars and habitual thieves. When missionary Francois Coillard first explained the commandment 'Thou shalt not steal' he found his audience in fits of laughter. On enquiring as to the reason for such mirth, a young man shouted gleefully,

'Oh missionary, you say stealing should be punished, but the whole country steals!'

Masters of weaving, their houses are made from papyrus matting, hung on a wooden frame and often of very intricate design. They are also good carvers and single pieces of wood with no joints are fashioned into dug-outs, dishes and bowls. They use hardwoods such as mukwa (*Pterocarpus angolensis*), mukushi (*Baikiaea plurijuga*) and mubako (*Erythrophloeum africanum*), found in the forests. They claim to be Christians, but most dare not ignore their traditional taboos and magic.

Barotsi life is dominated by the annual flooding of the Zambezi. The rains start in November. By the end of February the floodplain is inundated with water. The Lozi have adapted to this unique situation. For nine months of the year they live on the plains, their villages built on mounds and ridges. Their cattle graze on rich pastures from November to February when the rains bring a flush of new grass, and from April to July when the receding waters provide fresh green shoots. They plant gardens in the alluvial depressions, fertilized and watered by the flood. Planting is done in July and reaping completed by December. During low water they trawl for fish. As the levels rise and fall, fish traps and reed fences criss-cross the small channels. As the rising flood makes life uncomfortable, the Lozi move to the forest margins to plant their summer gardens.

The Kuomboka Ceremony

This yearly migration to the escarpment is the major event in the Lozi calendar. Led by the *litunga*, the ceremony is known as *Kuomboka*, meaning 'to get out of water'. The king and his household move from Lealui to the palace of Limilunga on the eastern escarpment. It is the largest tribal ceremony held in Africa. As the flood nears its peak, the date for *Kuomboka* is set to coincide with the rising moon and good omens. As communications are difficult throughout Zambia, it was more by luck than planning that we arrived in Mongu in time for the celebrations. We were fortunate to be there in a good flood year as the higher the flood, the grander the ceremony.

For two days the night air throbbed with the beat of the royal drums, *maoma*, summoning the paddlers to Lealui. These hollowed tree trunks, covered in taut animal hide, can be heard for 15 kilometres.

The morning of *Kuomboka* dawned. We carried our inflatable dinghy *Chikwekwe* down to the harbour as the sun was rising. The tortuous, 15-kilometre route through channels between banks of reeds and grass was lined with boats of every size and shape, all somewhat less seaworthy than our own.

The first *Kuombokas* took place in the early 19th century. A new barge (*nalikwanda*) was built for each occasion and materials were brought from different parts of the kingdom to signify unity. Although the word *nalikwanda* implies 'saving the people from drowning', the barges were far from watertight. King Lewanika was the most innovative of barge builders. He asked Coillard to show him the techniques of European ship-building and, in 1889, with the help of Waddell, the mission artisan, a barge was built *ka sikuwa* 'as the white man does'. The current *nalikwanda* was completed in 1984. It will be sunk on the death of the *litunga*, after transporting his body to the burial site. It is believed that the king lives in his ship in the watery underworld to which his spirit is consigned.

We walked towards the tall reed fence surrounding the palace courtyard. Bodyguards with *sjamboks* (long whips) patrolled the perimeters, lashing out at anyone who ventured too close. No-one may enter the courtyard. Women are particularly taboo.

It is an honour to be asked to be a paddler. Men travel from all over Zambia to accept the privilege. Ninety-six of them had collected under a shady tree near the enclosure, receiving instructions from the *induna* (chief). The *litunga* was due to appear at 10.00 am. It was now 11.00 am and the loading of the barge had not begun; time is elastic in Africa.

The royal procession

At last the palace stewards appeared, carrying the *litunga's* luggage. Maize meal, cooking pots, water jars, clothes, cushions and blankets were stowed under the canopy. Each item was presented to the packers with ritual bowing and clapping, a sign of respect for the king.

The paddlers gathered at Nyauma, the place of embarkation. A roll of drums heralded the appearance of the *litunga*. He wore a pale linen suit. One of his captains led him to the barge. The onlookers clapped and bowed, chanting, 'Yo-shoo!' Acknowledging the royal salute with a nod, he stepped aboard and disappeared beneath the canopy. The paddlers took their positions, and with a rhythmic drumbeat and much ululating from the banks, the *nalikwanda* edged into the main channel.

Nataikwa, a small canoe paddled by the *litunga's* bodyguard, and the only craft allowed to travel ahead of the king, led the royal barge out of the harbour. The procession gradually picked up speed and began its wide sweep behind the island where the queen's barge, *notila*, and other royal craft were waiting. People scrambled for places on their boats. With much jostling, they followed the rapidly disappearing *nalikwanda* in an untidy stream. The procession was joined by hundreds of small boats from the villages it passed. Goats and chickens huddled in the wobbling, overloaded dug-outs as they embarked on the perilous journey to the shore.

The sun was setting as the *nalikwanda* nosed her way into view. The barge approached the shore, then turned away. Three times she repeated this manoeuvre, each time to a different song. The crowd, now some 10,000 strong, pressed forward as she landed. The *litunga* appeared. His casual suit had been discarded and, resplendent in a British admiral's uniform, he was led to the palace. The uniform was given to King Lewanika in 1902, during his visit to England for the coronation of King Edward VII. It has been passed from *litunga* to *litunga* and has been used for *Kuomboka* ever since. Just outside the palace gates the celebrations had begun. A thud of bare feet and rythmic chanting rose from the courtyard.

The floodplain

The next day the harbour was deserted. A few old men sat with their legs in the water, nursing their hangovers. We launched *Chikwekwe* and set off to explore the floodplain. The bird life is abundant and accustomed to boats. We crept up on openbills and black-headed herons, who watched our approach, heads on one side, and flew off as we came within a few metres. African marsh harriers hovered over the reeds, their legs extended, waiting to swoop on an unsuspecting rodent or snake. The water currents are strong and variable. We heard several tales of dug-outs capsizing and their occupants drowning.

A large python battled across the swirling water and disappeared into the reeds. We saw no evidence of crocodiles or hippos. Apparently most of these are found in the main Zambezi channel, 30 kilometres into the swamp. Hippos used to be hunted with harpoons from dug-outs. The battles between man and beast were violent and evenly matched, but guns have altered the balance and their numbers have been heavily reduced. The hippopotamus is vital to the swamplands. Its movements keep the channels open, and its disappearance is thought to be contributing to the gradual clogging up of the floodplain.

In the quiet backwaters, carpets of waterlilies turned their pink and white faces to the sun. Fishermen baited their traps and trolled from their dug-outs. White-winged terns dipped into the water and flights of white-faced ducks and Egyptian and spurwinged geese circled overhead. Pied kingfishers hovered over the shallows, searching for fingerlings. Stonechats, orange-breasted waxbills, red bishops and many others clamoured on the reed-banks. Jan donned his wetsuit and disappeared with his underwater camera into the maze of aquatic plants. Staring in astonishment at the snorkled figure with orange flippers, a boat-load of passing Lozi hit a tree stump and almost capsized.

The Ngonye Falls

We left Mongu and drove down the eastern escarpment to Senanga. South of this small town the margins of the floodplain meet. We bumped slowly across the tail of the swamp, between narrow channels criss-crossed by fish fences.

At last we reached the Zambezi, only to find that the ferry had dropped a cement truck into the mud. We waited, passing the time bird-watching and reading. Six hours later, an army ferry came to our rescue and we were dumped, unceremoniously, on the other side.

The river, sometimes nearly two kilometres wide, flows through undulating woodland, over several shallow rapids, towards Katimo Mulilo. A hundred kilometres downstream of Senanga are the Ngonye Falls. Once known as the Sioma Falls, this horseshoe-shaped cataract is formed by a wall of basalt 25 metres high, creating a series of widely spreading cascades. Even today, they have been visited by only a handful of people.

We clambered over the basalt, eroded and polished by the surging water into a myriad of forms. The fine, white sand between the rocks squeaked as we walked. We longed for a swim off one of the beaches, but the unpredictable currents and signs of crocodile activity kept us from plunging in.

Below the Ngonye gorge the river widens again and the chain of cataracts is formidable. The Lusu, commonly referred to as the 'death rapids', are notorious, having claimed several lives among the early explorers. This part of the river is also renowned for its crocodiles. The natives claim that these reptiles acquired a taste for man in the days of Sepopa, when human offenders were fed to them. The man-eaters have obviously been heavily persecuted in the interim for we saw no signs of their existence. The area is sparsely habited with forests of mukushi *(Baikiaea plurijuga)*, mukwa *(Pterocarpus angolensis)*, marula*(Sclerocarya caffra)* and numerous other trees growing on the acid, grey sand veld.

German legacy

The town of Katima Mulilo, situated beside a stretch of rapids, was established as the seat of rule for the eastern Caprivi Strip in 1890. This finger of land, some 300 kilometres long and 50 kilometres in width, was given to the Germans by the British in 1890, in exchange for Zanzibar. Named after the Chancellor of Germany at the time, Count von Caprivi, it allowed the Germans access to the Zambezi river. They erroneously believed this would give them a trade route across Africa. As is so often the case in African history, the strip defies geographic, ethnographic and economic logic and has been a constant source of dispute.

Habitation increases from Katima Mulilo to the old town of Mwandi. In 1944 this village was moved to the healthier, more picturesque site of Sesheke. The area is flat and fertile, susceptible to annual flooding by the Zambezi. The natives grow maize, millet, pumpkins, cassava and beans. There are few roads and the river is used as a highway between the scattered villages.

Swamplands

Beyond Mwandi, the steep banks fade into the 'Caprivi swamps'. The river meanders between floating islands of reeds, sedges and kazungula grass *(Setaria sphacelata)*. In the quiet backwaters, mahogany-coloured curtains of the aquatic fern *(Azolla pinnata)* hang between masses of floating water lettuce *(Pistia stratiotes)*. This small lily traps air in the dense mat of hair covering its yellow-green leaves, enabling it to bob up to the surface whenever submerged. Gliding through the verdant vegetation and quiet waterways are numerous *makoros* (dug-outs). The long poles are pulled rhythmically, the paddlers never forgetting the age-old African maxim, 'He who digs his pole too deep will be stuck forever.'

The swamplands are formed by the flooding of the Zambezi and Kwando rivers. During a normal rainy season about 40 percent of the area between these two rivers is submerged. For six years during the 1980s the region experienced the worst drought in recorded history. Large stretches of wetland were replaced by rolling grasslands. Settlements encroached onto the floodplains. Rice paddy schemes, schools and roads were built. The rivers will flood again and man will be pushed back to the swamp margins once more, but meanwhile the drought has enabled organized poaching to reach this once inaccessible wilderness. Buffalo, lechwe and impala were shot in their hundreds. Efforts are being made to designate parts of the area as game reserve, but they may be too late.

Where four countries meet

Near Kazangula, the pale blue waters of the Chobe join the deep indigo of the Zambezi. In the middle of the river is a small island, Konkumba, where the corners of four countries, Zimbabwe, Zambia, Botswana and Namibia, converge. Stories tell of a trader who lived here for many years carrying on his business unhampered by government laws.

'Prove the island is yours and I will pay immediately', he would retort to any demands for taxes or licence fees. The question of ownership remains unsettled.

Kazungula, a small border town on the Zambezi south bank, marks the official boundary between the four countries. Just outside the village stands the famous 'Kazungula tree', where Livingstone spent the night on his way to the Falls. It is a large *Kigelia africana*, or sausage tree, named because of its unusual shaped fruits. Africans hang these fruits in their huts as a charm against whirlwinds.

Until the break up of The Federation[1], Kazungula was an important cattle-crossing. The herds were driven, often 400 or 500 kilometres, from ranches in Botswana to the growing markets in Zambia. The river crossing was made with the aid of a flat-bottomed barge. Twenty head of cattle would be driven into the water, tied to the boat and forced to swim across.

The swamplands end abruptly about 20 kilometres downstream from Kazungula. The meandering Zambezi encounters the Katambora rapids, over a kilometre of swirling white water, and is trapped again between rolling sand scarps.

The waters calm once more. The river, in many places more than a kilometre wide, is studded with islands. Many are simply small sand-bars covered in reeds and wild willow trees, while the larger support dense riparian woodland. We explored the channels and backwaters between the islets, nosing our way gently around corners, our eyes peeled for any somnolent hippo; *Chikwekwe* could quite easily be deflated by one of their giant canines. We crept up on a small heronry. White-breasted cormorants and purple herons jostled and grumbled at our approach, but soon returned to the busy task of tending their young.

It is evening. Golden light filters through the dum palms *(Hyphaene ventricosa)*, their fan-like heads stark against the magenta sky. A formation of little egrets skim overhead, elephants drink greedily in the shallows and baboons clamour and squabble as they climb to their favourite roosts. A subterranean rumble echoes in the distance, carried for a moment on a gust of wind.

1. **Federation** — of Rhodesia (Northern and Southern) and Nyasaland. After its dissolution in 1963, Northern Rhodesia was to become Zambia, Southern Rhodesia to become Rhodesia (now Zimbabwe), and Nyasaland to become Malawi.

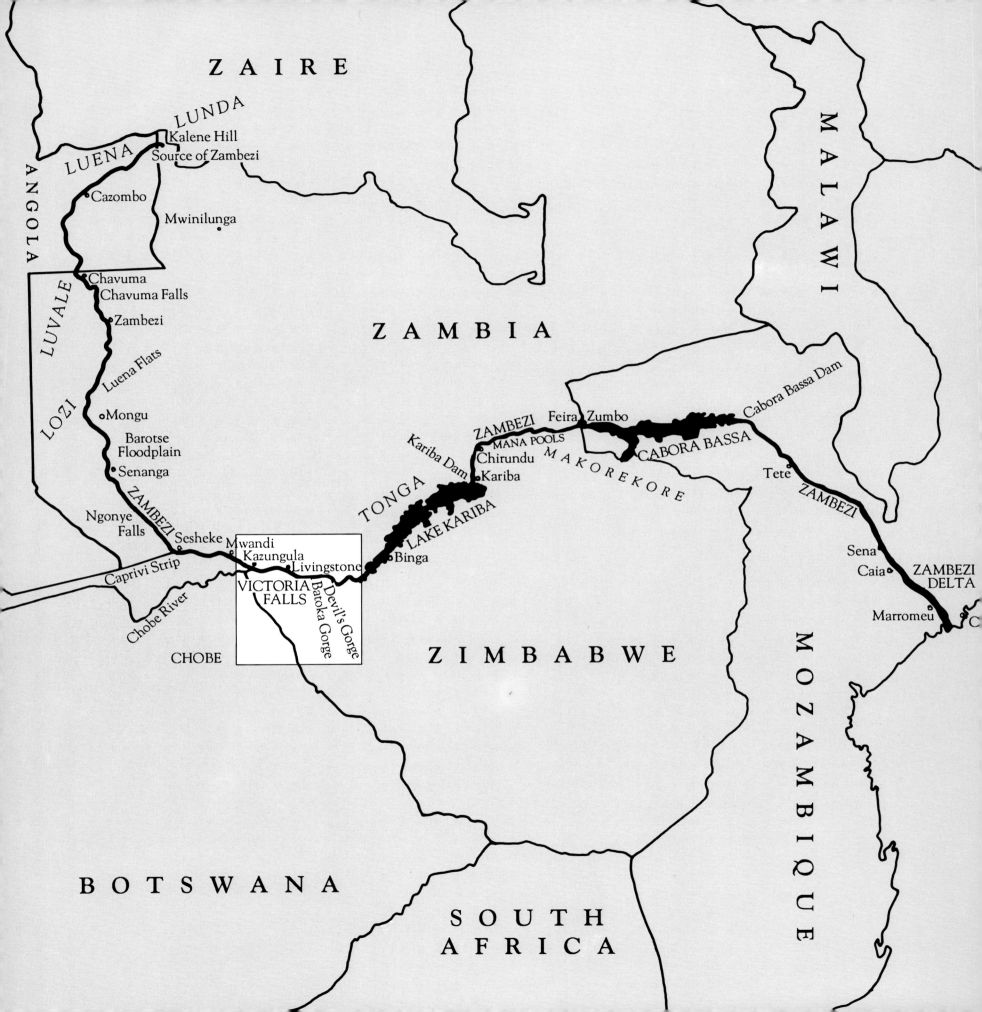

VICTORIA FALLS

An almost continuous record of man's evolution over the last two million years in the form of tools has been preserved in the sands and gravels of the Victoria Falls area. The earliest examples are just pebbles with a small flake chipped off for cutting and scraping. The Middle and Late Stone Ages brought blades, axes, barbs and arrowheads, followed by the iron hoes and spearheads of the Iron Age traditions.

The bushmen were doubtless the first people aquainted with the Falls. Around 1500 AD the Tonga-Ila peoples arrived in the area. Peaceful agriculturalists with a knowledge of iron and clay working, these early Tonga lived in small farming communities, mingling and inter-marrying with the bushmen. They knew the Falls as *shongwe*, 'a seething cauldron'. Cataract and Goat Islands, on the lip of the chasm, were used as places of worship. Here they built their spirit huts, *kaanda*, in view of the rainbows, and sacrificed animals into the raging torrent to pacify the rain god, Basungu. Their Makololo conquerors named the Falls *Mosi-oa-tunya*, or 'the smoke that thunders'. On 23rd November 1855, Livingstone, accompanied by Chief Sekelutu's Makololo paddlers landed on Goat island (now Livingstone Island) on the tip of the chasm.

'At one time,' wrote Livingstone later, 'we seemed to be going right into the gulf but, though I felt a little tremor, I said nothing believing I could face the difficulty as well as my guides.'

It was the only time in his life that the explorer deviated from his rule of retaining the African place name, and instead claimed the Falls for England and named them after his queen.

Apart from Silva Porto[1] and Lazslo Magyar[2], historians have put forward several Arabs, Portuguese and Boer hunters as the first outsiders to witness the spectacular phenomenon of the Falls. If they were, their discovery cannot be of any more consequence than that of the Tonga or the Makololo. For it was Livingstone who was their illuminator, the first to bring their splendour to the attention of the outside world. It is with his name that this, one of the seven wonders of the world, is most frequently associated.

1. **Antonio Francisco Ferreira da Silva Porto** — 19th century Portuguese trader who pioneered ivory trade routes from the Atlantic coast to the Zambezi and Congo basins.

2. **Lazslo Magyar** 1817-64, Hungarian explorer who journeyed from the Angolan port of Benguela eastwards to the Upper Zambezi basin 1849-57.

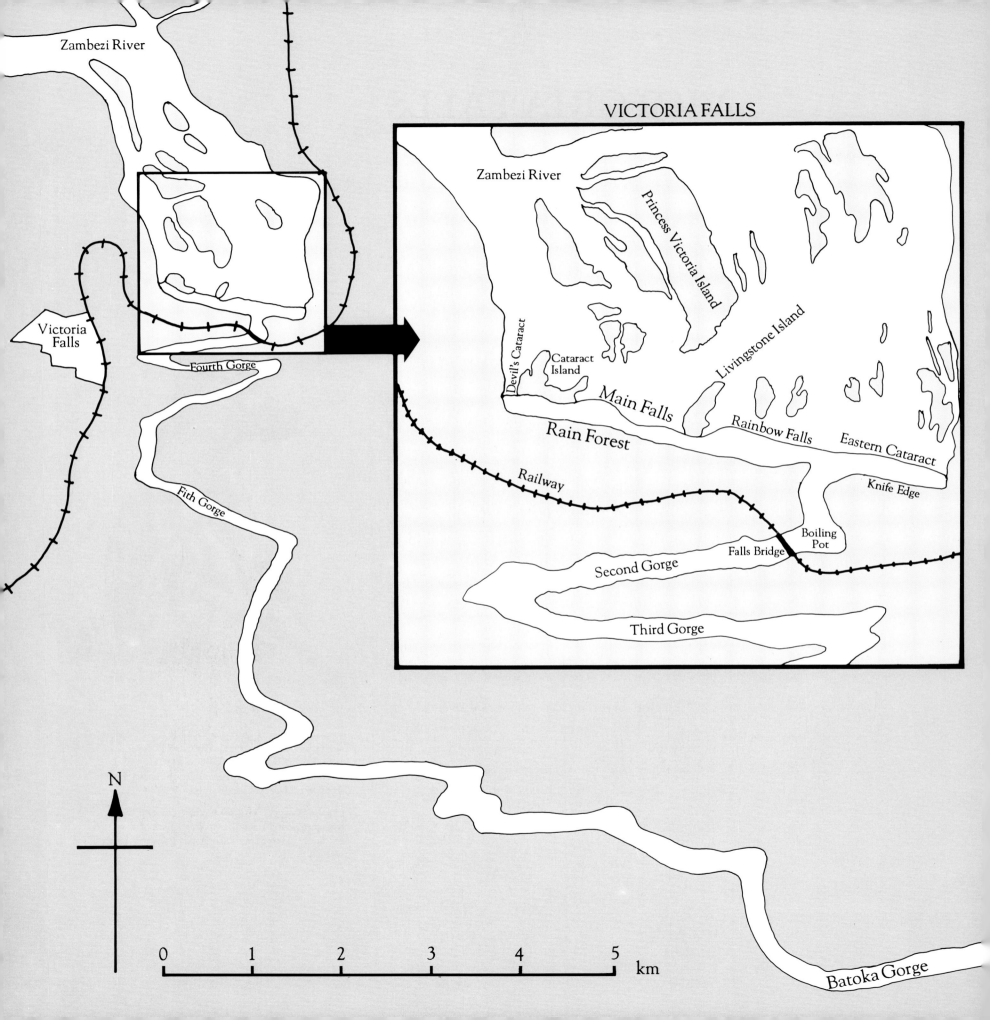

Zambezi River

Victoria
Falls

Fourth Gorge

Fith Gorge

N

0   1   2   3   4   5   km

VICTORIA FALLS

Zambezi River

Princess Victoria Island

Devil's Cataract

Cataract Island

Livingstone Island

Main Falls

Rain Forest

Rainbow Falls

Eastern Cataract

Knife Edge

Railway

Boiling Pot

Falls Bridge

Second Gorge

Third Gorge

Batoka Gorge

Formation of the Falls

Early explorers believed that the cataract was the result of a cataclysmic shattering of the earth's crust, creating the chasm into which the Zambezi waters now drop. Geological studies have proved this theory incorrect. The Victoria Falls, like most waterfalls, have been formed by the relentless erosive action of moving water.

Some 150 million years ago, molten lava oozed out of cracks in the earth's surface, in a series of giant flows, each settling and cooling on the last. Bubbles of water vapour escaped from the surfaces of the solidifying deposits, creating red, reticulated bands of basalt, sandwiched between blue fine-grained layers. The rock hardened and contracted, leaving a network of deep fissures. The larger of these cracks form a series of major east-west 'joints', linked together by smaller north-south clefts. With the passage of time these faults were filled with soft limestone deposits.

Many geologists believe that the upper Zambezi was once an entirely separate river, flowing south-east through the Makgadikgadi depression in northern Botswana and possibly joining the Limpopo system on the southern border of Zimbabwe. Gentle movements in the earth's crust, about two million years ago, are thought to have cut off the Zambezi's access to the sea, resulting in a huge inland lake, the remains of which include the Okovango Delta, the Chobe Swamps and the Makgadikgadi salt pans. Spillage from these wetlands ran over onto the low-lying area to the east, carving a new river valley through the wind-blown Kalahari sands deposited on the basalt sediments.

The headwaters of the middle and lower Zambezi were thought to have been the Matetsi river, approximately 100 kilometres downstream from the Falls of today. The Matetsi ran in a deep valley, the western scarp formed by the edge of the basalt 'plate'. The upper river, following its new course, tumbled over this 250-metre drop, creating the first 'Victoria Falls'. It joined the waters of the middle Zambezi, so forming the river system as we know it today.

The pounding water found a weakness in one of the large east-west fissures in the basalt. The erosive process began, washing away the soft limestone deposits and cleaving out the Batoka Gorge. About eight kilometres downstream from the Falls the river swings north. With the change in direction of the waterflow, the erosion also altered, digging back along a short north-south fissure. This linked with another east-west cleft. Gradually a broad waterfall was excavated across the river. The process was repeated, resulting in a zig-zag pattern of gorges, eight in all. Today's fall line, in the first of these gorges, is probably some 2500 years old. The lip of the Falls is showing two points of recession, the larger on the western side of Cataract Island, the second through Livingstone Island. The retreat of the Falls continues.

Early settlers

Numerous exploration parties followed Livingstone, but it was not until 40 years later that the discovery of the Hwange coal fields in Zimbabwe, and the presence of rich copper deposits in the Kafue region of Zambia, brought the first settlers. These findings altered Cecil John Rhodes'[1] plan for the Cape to Cairo railway, re-routeing it to link Bulawayo with the coal fields and the copper mines. There was one major obstacle — the Zambezi. In 1898 a wagon-road was cut from Bulawayo and a regular coach service set up. A steady traffic of mining personnel, prospectors, hunters and traders bumped uncomfortably across the veld for 12 dusty days. They were ferried across the river nine kilometres above the Falls.

The crossing was controlled by 'Mopane' Clarke, the first permanent settler in the region. On a flat, marshy site on the north bank he set up three stores, an hotel and a bar. His iron barge, propelled by eight Barotse paddlers, plied backwards and forwards across the river. By 1903 the Old Drift settlement had a population of 68, with Clarke as a kind of honorary Lord Mayor. The bar stayed open all night. One shilling bought a whisky and soda and the roulette wheel was kept spinning.

The silent creeks and reed-beds surrounding the settlement bred mosquitoes in vast numbers. In spite of ample quantities of quinine, malaria was rampant. After the only doctor and the two pharmacists succumbed to blackwater fever, the administrative offices were moved to 'Constitution Hill', a sand belt on the Zambian side, where Livingstone town stands today. With the arrival of the railway on the Zambezi south bank in 1904, the fate of the original settlement was sealed.

Crossing point

A bridge was needed to ford the Zambezi. The site was chosen by Rhodes, who never visited the river and died two years before construction began. He demanded that it be built just below the Falls, so that the spray would soak the railway carriages. His will prevailed and created one of the most spectacular border crossings in the world.

The 60-metre bridge was constructed from each side of the narrow gorge at the western end of the Falls, through which the Zambezi waters escape. To avoid the 12-kilometre journey from one bank to the other, a bosun's chair was used, which consisted of a wooden seat with a canvas back hung by four ropes from a cable . A safety net, 90 metres above the water, was suspended across the gorge. On first seeing the net the entire native work force went on strike, thinking they would be compelled to leap into it!

---

1. **Cecil John Rhodes** — (1853-1902) Statesman and empire builder. Founded de Beers Mining Company in 1880. In 1890 became Prime Minister of Cape Province. Responsible for the exploration and development of Rhodesia.

The two parts were finally bolted together early on the morning of 1st April 1905, before the metal could expand in the heat of the sun. It was no April Fool. To the disappointment of local cartoonists, the two parts slotted together perfectly. The Zambezi had been spanned for the first time. The bridge was then the highest in the world and had been completed in a record 14 months. In 1904 the wooden shack erected to house the workers was converted into the famous Victoria Falls Hotel, which is a thriving tourist attraction to this day.

Livingstone town grew rapidly. In 1907 it became the capital of northwestern Rhodesia and, in 1911, of the whole of Northern Rhodesia. The World Cup sculling championships, held above the Falls in 1910, marked its place in the sporting history books. However, in 1935 the seat of government was moved to Lusaka and the town's boom years were over. In 1965 Southern Rhodesia declared independence. The border was closed and Livingstone, no longer able to function as a trade link, became little more than a tourist centre.

Diesel and electric trains have not yet superseded steam engines, which chuff across the bridge carrying passengers and freight. The first natives to see these mechanical giants were terrified by the 'huge animal with only one eye'.

'It feeds on fire and hates work,' they said. 'When the white man pumps it to make it work, it screams.'

'It must have the fever very badly,' a young Ndebele observed, while watching an engine being serviced, ' the white man pours medicine on so many parts of its body.'

A steam-train fanatic can spend many an hour fuelling his passion as these beautifully maintained engines puff and hiss in and out of the old Victoria Falls station. Indeed for some visitors this is a special attraction.

The Falls are guarded by *Chipique,* **a ten-metre long, snake-like creature with a grey head and a thick black body, large enough to engulf a boat. Local fishermen say he appears in the dark hours to oversee his domain.**

The character of the Falls varies greatly with the time of year. In March and April more than a million gallons per second tumble into the gorge. Observers are drenched with the spray, which is so dense that most of the spectacle is hidden from view. In late November the water is carried over the lip in shimmering rivulets separated by expanses of dry black rock.

No safety rails or nets have been erected to prevent observers from falling over the edge, and one may paddle in a canoe as close to the brink as one dares. Trooper Ramsay, who was stationed in the area, had a lucky escape in 1904. He lost his paddle while kayaking above the Falls and was washed over into the Boiling Pot. A policeman, idling on the edge of Danger Point watched, horrified, as canoe and body parted company and the craft shattered on the rocks below. He managed to scramble down the precipice and catch the motionless figure before it was washed away in the current, and was amazed to find Ramsay unconscious but alive, having incurred no injuries apart from numerous bruises and a bump on the head.

An elderly and somewhat intoxicated gentleman fell over the edge while stumbling home in the dark one night. He plummeted into the chasm, but was miraculously caught in a tree growing at right angles to the cliff face. When rescued the following morning, he seemed oblivious of his near-fatal fall, complaining only about the loss of his false teeth and the bottle of Scotch he had been clutching!

Others have not been so lucky. A young man was found one day in a sitting position on a ledge below Knife Edge; he was dead. Apart from a train ticket in his pocket he carried no other documents and was never identified.

The rain forest

The rain forest is not a true tropical rain forest, but an extension of the fringing vegetation found along the river banks. On the edge of the spray zone the dry Mopane scrub suddenly changes. Muchenja or African ebony, muchiningi *(Mimusops zeyheri)*, mukuyu or the Cape fig, Natal mahogany *(Trichilia emetica)* and a variety of other species form a dense green canopy. The trees are festooned with woody creepers and twisted vines. The wailing cry of trumpeter hornbills, hidden in the foliage, rises over the thunder of the cataract. Dozens of wild date palms *(Phoenix reclinata)* scatter their graceful fronds over the ground. Herbaceous flowers abound between the numerous ferns and mosses. The most spectacular of these is the blood-lily *(Haemanthus multiflorus)*. Its brilliant red inflorescence dominates the undergrowth through the early summer months. Bushbuck forage in the rich grasses, their dappled coats blending into the shadows. Snails slither along the fallen branches in search of food and frogs chirp noisily. The forest provides a unique ecological home for thousands of species.

The Zambezi escapes the first gorge through a narrow gap between two promontories, Danger Point and Knife Edge. In the whirling Boiling Pot below, the waters flowing east from Devil's Cataract, the Main Falls and the Rainbow Falls meet the westward torrent from the Eastern Cataract.

Riding the rapids

The easiest way to follow the zig-zag pattern of the gorges is by means of a rubber boat specially built for shooting rapids. This part of the river offers some of the most exciting wild-water sport in the world. It is graded five in rafting terminology (six is unrunnable). It is certainly a sport upon which the adrenalin addict can thrive.

We floated gently on the oily calm, the sound of rushing water growing louder as the current carried us downstream. High above us two black eagles circled lazily on the thermals. Fever trees (*Commiphora marlothii*) with their bright, greenish yellow bark, clung to the dark gorge walls. A Tonga fisherman watched us pass, leaning against a boulder at the entrance to his cave, indifferent to our presence. A hand-line hung limply by his side and the basket at his feet was empty. It is a harsh, lonely existence ekeing out a living from this inhospitable environment.

We slipped around a corner, the water starting to churn against the sides of the raft. Ahead of us was a foaming torrent, broken by an untidy chain of jagged rocks.

'High-side. Low-side. Push onto the waves. Don't let go of the ropes,' barked the oarsman.

We hung on. For an instant we teetered on the edge. The Avon dinghy tipped gently into the maelstrom of water, which crashed over our heads as we were tossed from wave to wave. We opened our eyes to see ahead of us a long stretch of calm. It was over! We started to bale out the water, the sun hot on our backs. The next rapid could be heard roaring ahead and we looked forward to it with a now familiar sense of pleasant trepidation. We were hooked.

Beyond the eighth canyon the Zambezi swings eastward into the Batoka Gorge. The vertical walls become shallower and the surrounding country more rugged, dissected by numerous steep tributary valleys. Most is accessible only on foot and much of it has never been explored. There are numerous rapids, the most spectacular of which are the Chimamba, or Moemba, Falls. This S-shaped cataract constricts the entire volume of the river into a channel 15 metres wide. The rock shudders with the force of churning water and a small rainbow hangs in the shower of spray.

The Zambezi continues to erode its gorge. At the Falls it is about 110 metres deep, while at its eastern end it reaches a depth of 350 metres. At low water, banks of basalt rubble are exposed. Huge potholes have been gouged into some of the larger sheets by the drilling action of small rocks, tumbled over and over by the rushing water. The natives say these are dinosaur footprints, left behind by the giant, prehistoric beasts as they fled from the oozing lava.

Crocodiles nesting

A few kilometres above the Matetsi confluence the basalt gives way to sandstone. The river widens and slows. Exposed sandbars provide favourite nesting sites for crocodiles. In August the female digs a deep hole in which she lays about 45 white eggs. She covers them with sand, gently packing it down with her hind legs. For 90 days she guards the nest from the water. The baby crocodiles begin to hatch, their throaty squeaks summoning their mother. She scrapes away the sand and, picking up the young in her mouth, transports them to the water's edge. About 20 centimetres long, they are perfect replicas of their adult counterparts and can swim immediately. The remaining eggs are rolled delicately between her powerful jaws to stimulate hatching.

These aggressive monsters of folklore are transformed into the gentlest of mothers. But maternal instincts cannot protect the young from predators. The eggs are a feast for leguvaans and baboons; the hatchlings a delicacy for herons, tigerfish and even other crocodiles. Only a tiny fraction survive, of which some may grow up to 4000 times their birthweight.

The gorge walls give way to flat-topped hills covered by mopane woodland. Villages are scattered along the banks. From the air a column of white spray rises into the sky 100 kilometres away to the west. We leave the Victoria Falls behind as we follow the Zambezi into the Gwembe Valley, the headwaters of Lake Kariba.

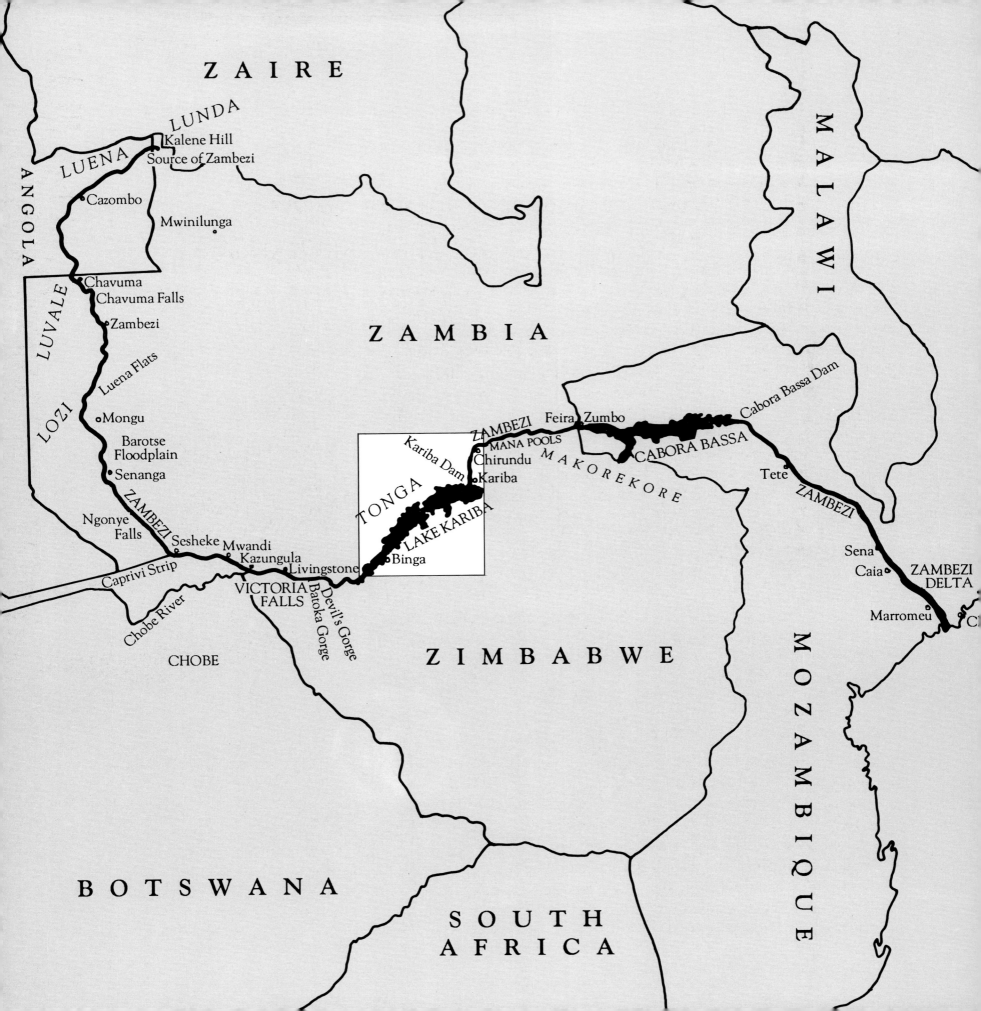

LAKE KARIBA

Life is hard for the Tonga, one of Africa's most primitive tribes. Sentiment is the preserve of the rich. Theirs is a world of dreams, of long-dead ancestors inhabiting baobab trees, of rainmakers and river gods, and witches straddling the backs of hyenas, bent upon missions of assassination and betrayal. Some years the rains are good and the grain bins full, but in others the rain shrine fails and the people go hungry. The old women smoke hubble-bubble pipes made from gourds and filled with dagga (*Cannabis sativa*). They wear red ochre in their hair and sticks through holes in their noses formed in their youth by piercing the nostrils with a thorn. Toothless gums attest to the *Kulangwa* ceremony, in which the four front teeth were chiselled out to enhance the beauty of teenage girls.

This custom has now been forbidden by law, but otherwise the Tonga people have changed little since Livingstone explored this area in 1855. They no longer slap their thighs and roll upon the ground in greeting, but clothing is almost as sparse as it was a century ago. It is hot here; in winter hot and dry and in summer hotter still, and wet. In winter the earth is brown and parched.

Fingers of cloud appear over the horizon and retreat before the scorching sun. The people beat their drums and gaze expectantly into the clear skies. The days grow longer. Late one afternoon, black clouds roll in and the rains come, sometimes 15 centimetres or more in a night. Crops are destroyed, huts are flattened and the people huddle together miserably. Then the sun comes out and steams everything dry. The temperature rises to 40°C, or even 45°C, and the rain falls again. The woodland becomes jungle, alive with the cries of birds and insects, but the river in the ravine is silent and lonely.

The villages of Batoka Gorge

We were exploring the Batoka Gorge area and travelling through the villages beyond the escarpment. Dyasabello, an old man with an inexhaustible fund of stories, had become our interpreter and friend. He had learned to speak English while working on the coal mine in Hwange some years before. Our presence in the area naturally stirred up the placid lives of the villagers and curious eyes followed us everywhere.

On arrival at any village, the headman would be waiting to greet us with elaborate courtesy. The best stools would be brought and placed beneath a shady tree, and a ritual

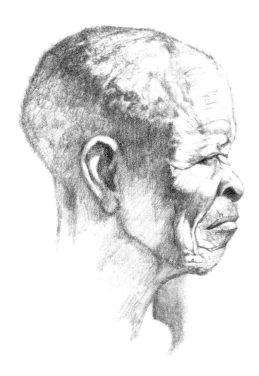

discussion about the latest problems held. It might be that a young girl was pregnant; or a man in the neigbouring village had lost three goats to crocodiles; or he, headman of the village, was involved in a dispute with his son-in-law over the question of *lobola* (dowry); or perhaps the rains had not been good, and then again would we buy him a wireless when next in Hwange? In the meantime, he would be grateful for a snap of himself and his family. We carried a polaroid camera and were always able to fulfil this last request. They showed no surprise when their image appeared on paper a minute later.

They would demonstrate their skills in basket-weaving and pottery, and show us their grain-storage houses made of clay and thatch and placed on stilts to guard against floods. Their little mud houses were pleasant and cool. The walls were decorated with pictures of plants and fish. They were simple dwellings, clustered beneath the hills like colonies of birds' nests, a little tattered by the end of the season, but easily rebuilt once new thatching grass had grown and dried. Chickens and children scuttled about in equal numbers. Women pounded corn and men sat and drank it in the form of beer. Everyone was cheerful. Wanting to shoot a portrait of a little girl, we produced a Hasselblad camera with a strange looking bellows attachment. The child ran away screaming and even the men looked disconcerted, thinking it was some sort of weapon. We resorted to 35mm cameras, which made everyone feel happier, for the better travelled men had seen these before.

One day we were taken to a funeral. Over the throb of drums and the chants of the dancers, the old man explained the significance of this event. The Tonga believe implicitly in the continued life of the departed. When someone dies, his soul is inherited by a living person, who takes on both the rights and obligations of the deceased. If it is a man's soul, the inheritor might take over his wives and become responsible for his offspring. If some of the children happen to be daughters, the heir may claim the *lobola*.

A daily hazard

While camped at the mouth of the Batoka Gorge, we were disturbed one sultry afternoon by a commotion down by the river. Heaving ourselves out of our hammocks, we rushed down to the water's edge to see what was afoot. A crocodile had taken one of the native cows. Dyasyabello, together with a number of children, was pelting it with rocks. The reptile relinquished its grip and the cow was saved. The next day brought a more tragic incident. The same crocodile took a nine-year-old girl as she was washing in the river. Onlookers heard a single, strangled shriek and she was gone. The story was never reported. It happens frequently in these remote areas, and the people accept such tragedies with a calm fatalism. It is just one of the ordinary hazards of life.

'Goats are taken almost every day in October and November, when they graze on the riverbank' said the old man.

He went on to describe how a livestock owner would stretch a goatskin with a bell around its neck over a bamboo frame. The dummy would be staked out in the current. A crocodile, attracted by the bell, might seize the decoy, which would collapse under the pressure of its jaws. If the skin was wet enough, it clogged up the crocodile's air passages, drowning it. We were a little dubious about this deterrent, but he assured us that the reptile, once it had a good hold, would not let go even though it drowned in the process.

Unwelcome resettlement

To a westerner, the trauma of moving from one county or state to another is bearable but for the Tonga it is unthinkable. Such was the tragedy of the Kariba Basin when, in 1954, the decision to dam the Zambezi at Kariba Gorge had been taken. It was to create an expanse of water the size of Wales, stretching the equivalent distance of London to Manchester or New York to Washington, making it by far the largest man-made lake in the world. But there were 57,000 Tonga tribesmen living on the intended site and the unpleasant task of moving them lay with Iain Cockroft and other District Commissioners (DCs). How were they to explain a hydro-electric power scheme to people who had never seen a light bulb?

For 60 years the Tonga of the Kariba Basin had led untroubled lives. British rule had put an end to the Matabele raids, and the yoke of the great English queen was not an onerous one. They saw her majesty's representative just once a year, when the DC for their area patrolled down the river in his motor boat. He was the only white man they ever saw, apart from the occasional hunter or prospector. The queen did not, apparently, want to take their cattle or enslave their children. On the contrary, the DC tried to help them with their problems and they looked forward to his visits.

The exodus of the Tonga before the flood was a pathetic story, a tragedy without a villain, unless industrial progress is to be cast in that role. Throughout the dry season of 1955, Cockroft and other DCs patrolled the valley on foot, patiently explaining the forthcoming event. Floods — yes, the people could understand that — and if the DC said there was to be a flood, he was probably right. The white man's medicine was strong and he might well know of these things. When it came, they would go up into the hills and return when the waters had subsided. But they were told that the flood would stay forever. The elders shook their heads. When the rains stopped, they said, the water would go down. After months of patient explanation, Cockroft thought he had made some progress. The

Mr Vulture was a great friend of Mr and Mrs Tortoise, whom he often visited. But Mr Tortoise, lacking wings, was upset that he was unable to return these visits. He thought at length about the problem and eventually had an idea.

'Tie me up in this bundle,' he said to his wife, 'when Vulture visits, tell him it is a lump of tobacco and ask him to use it to buy grain for us.'

Mr Vulture arrived, and Mrs Tortoise, telling him of the grain shortage, begged him to trade the tobacco for a little food. Vulture accepted at once, picked up the parcel in his talons and flew back to his home in the heights.

As they were nearing the lofty citadel Mr.Tortoise called out from the bag, 'Untie me Vulture! It is I, Tortoise. I have come to visit you!' Vulture was so surprised that he dropped the parcel, and Tortoise was smashed into a thousand pieces.

That is why Vulture and Tortoise are no longer friends, and why Tortoise has so many cracks in his shell.

The soul walks like a shadow behind its caretaker, who must attend to its every whim. When the caretaker dies he passes to the next-in-line both his own soul and the attendant spirit, so that in time a man may aquire a collection of souls.

To ensure that this train does not become too unwieldy, long-dead ancestors are dropped out of the shadow after a few generations and take up residence in a tree, usually a baobab. The tree forms an integral part of village life and generations of tribesmen look forward to joining their ancestors among its boughs in the distant future. They are at one with the earth and the village forms the centre of their world. Time has no meaning. The dead and yet unborn mingle happily with the living in the village square.

Tonga trusted him and seemed prepared to move. Heavy rains fell in the valley that year, roads became impassable and the Tonga were cut off from the world.

In May 1956, when Cockroft ventured in again, he found a marked change of attitude. Younger members of the tribe had begun stirring up dissent. The subject had been debated to the exclusion of all else in the intervening months. Although the villagers had been promised a new way of life and were to be given schools and hospitals, food, irrigation schemes, markets for their crops and fishing rights on the new lake, the reality was rather different. They were to be thrust abruptly into a civilization about which they knew nothing. Young Tonga tribesmen said that the lake story was simply a white man's plot to oust them from their lands, and they were unenthusiastic about the Utopia that had been offered to them. For city dwellers the Zambezi was a natural barrier dividing two countries, but to the Tonga there had never been such frontiers. And what of the dead living in their ancestral trees? They might drown. Even if they could be induced to abandon their resting places, was there any guarantee that they would find their way to the new homes? The river had immense spiritual significance and was the focal point around which their lives revolved. Surely Nyaminyami, the river god, would not allow the white man to destroy his domain?

'Let them try,' they said, 'the river will push the wall over. The white man does not understand its power.'

Tonga etiquette holds that it is courteous to agree with a superior, even if his remarks are clearly nonsense. Cockroft patiently described the wall and its effects on their lives. They listened politely, asked questions and agreed to his suggestions.

The governments hoped that they would not have to use force and in order to make the move as easy as possible, land was found in remote, uninhabited corners of the valley which would not be lost to the rising waters. Large numbers of animals, especially elephant, were shot, until the survivors moved out of the designated areas. Encouraged by the help of a protracted medical campaign which effected seemingly miraculous cures of the diseases and malnourishment so prevalent among them, the Tonga on the Southern Rhodesian side (now Zimbabwe) accepted their lot and grudgingly left their homes. Eventually all on the southern side and most on the north bank were resettled without casualties.

Group resistance

One group of 6000, however, clung tenaciously to the river bank. They were chief Chipepo's people, occupying good land on the more heavily populated Zambian side. Adjacent land could not be found for them and they were to be moved to Lusitu, 160 kilometres down the river. Chipepo's people owned 3800 head of cattle and they worried

that the proposed site might be infested with the tsetse fly and that their livestock would be destroyed. If the new land was so fertile, why was nobody living there? And how were the ancestors to be moved? This problem had been overcome in other villages by cutting a branch from the ancestral tree and dragging it behind the truck in which they were transported. The departed had ridden along on the boughs of the tree, remaining in contact with the ground on the way to the new dwelling place. But it was clearly impractical to drag trees as far as Lusitu.

The Federal Governments had made plans to use the lake for commercial fishing. Substantial areas were to be cleared of trees and other obstacles to make way for gill nets. The largest bulldozers ever made were linked together with battleship chain, interspersed with huge steel balls. They drove on parallel courses through the forest, dragging the chains in loops behind them. Each team of two managed to clear an average of 30 acres an hour. The speed with which the land was devastated shocked even the Europeans working on the scheme, and the Tonga were horrified. They had never seen a gill net, but they knew about land clearing. It was done in order to plant crops and this confirmed their belief that the lake story was subterfuge.

Chipepo's people had not moved by December 1957, when phenomenal rains fell. The Zambezi flooded up its own tributaries, circling behind the hills, washing away whole villages and turning forests into swamps. The waters rose with astonishing rapidity. A crocodile, attracted by the bleating of a goat, swam into one village. In a vain attempt to protect his animal, the owner dragged it into one of the flooded huts. The crocodile swam right through the door and instead of taking the goat, seized the man and carried him off into the swamp before the horrified eyes of onlookers. The villagers were forced into the hills, their crops gone, huddling in wretched groups and living on roots and berries. No trucks could be moved in to evacuate them and many of the elderly died. The waters subsided in April, but still Chipepo's people opted to stay.

A matter of honour

The old war drums, idle for three quarters of a century, were taken out and dusted and before long rythmic messages were being pounded from village to village. The call could not be ignored. Old men and boys sharpened their spears and axes and began practising war manoeuvres. One day the DC of the area, Alex Smith, stopped his Landrover beside an old man he knew well.

'Greetings Davy,' he said. The old man took off his leopard-skin hat and, smiling, returned the greeting. The DC had nicknamed him 'Davy Crocket' because of his hat,

Nyaminyami is a serpent-like creature. He is about three metres wide, but nobody can guess at his length. The water stains red when he swims past. He has scales and a human face. Chief Sampakaruma saw him on two occasions many years ago, but the river god has been in hiding since the white men arrived in the country. He lived under a large rock close to the present dam wall. No tribesman ventured near it. Those few who did were sucked down with their canoes in the whirlpools and never seen again. They called the rock Kariwa, *the trap, and hence the name of the lake, Kariba.*

which was worn night and day. They exchanged the usual pleasantries about each others' health.

'And where might you be going?' asked Smith, eyeing the bundle of war spears the old man carried.

'To the war.'

'Don't be silly. You're too old for that kind of nonsense.'

'I know.'

'Who are you planning to fight anyway?'

'You, I think,' replied the old man, and went on his way, chuckling delightedly. The DC could not really believe the peace-loving Tonga were serious.

Tension grew. A police unit was called in. The villages were empty except for women and small children, who were frightened and bewildered. It was a farcical situation, with the Tonga posturing and practising mock attacks while the police, eyeing them from an adjoining hill, drilled their men and blew their bugles. If it were not for the tragic outcome this could have been a scene from a Shakespearean comedy.

At dawn on 10th September 1958, police surrounded the first of the villages to be moved. They were charged by about 100 spearmen. Tear-gas was fired from a distance of 50 metres but the warriors kept coming, hurling their spears. The police opened fire. Eight tribesmen were killed and 34 wounded. Among the dead, his leopard-skin hat lying to one side in a pool of blood, lay old Davy Crocket. The police were devastated. They had not meant this to happen. They had suffered no casualties, except for one minor wrist wound caused by a discharge from a fellow policeman's shotgun.

The tribesmen scattered into the bush where they remained in isolated bands for a few days before trickling back to their villages. They expressed surprisingly little rancour against the authorities, and appeared almost relieved that the matter had been settled. There could be no more resistance, but the debt of honour had been paid. They moved before the wall was sealed and their villages are now more than 30 metres underwater.

Revenge of the river god

City dwellers had mocked the stories of Nyaminyami, the Tonga river god. But by 1958 the laughter had turned to chilled apprehension, especially among those working on the project. Survey work on the proposed dam began in the late 1940s. On the night of 15th February 1950, a cyclone from the Indian Ocean swept up the valley. Such a thing had never been heard of in this landlocked, stable land. Fifteen inches of rain, driven by a hurricane, fell in a few hours. The river rose seven metres that night. A number of villages were swept away. When rescue teams finally managed to reach the area three days later, the putrefying bodies of antelope and other animals were seen hanging from the tops of trees. The survey team had perished in a landslide.

Work on the dam began in earnest in 1955. A difficult road was cut through the mountains to the gorge. Razor Ridge, Buffalo Nec, Kidney Hill, Puff Adder Ridge and Rhino Nec were some of the obstacles named by the road-building gang. One stretch of three kilometres, which no road engineer could bear to look at, was called Savory's Folly. But they won through in the end. Site huts were set up near the gorge and work on the coffer dam began.

On Christmas Eve, 1955, an unprecedented flood stormed down the gorge and washed away the foundations of the coffer dam and the recently constructed pontoon bridge. The flood peaked, receded, then peaked again. This had never happed before and the Tonga river god started to crop up in bar-room conversation.

The Italian consortium, Impresit, which had won the civil engineering tender for the construction of the dam, arrived in 1956. In November of that year, heavy rains fell a month before they were due. Sudden flash floods impeded work on the dam. The Zambezi, swollen with water from local catchment areas, would rise over a metre in a night. The Italians accepted this unusual weather with equanimity and found the stories of Nyaminyami merely entertaining.

They were unaware that 1300 kilometres away, the Zambezi was mobilizing its forces. It is fed by a catchment area of over a million square kilometres, of which nearly half is above the lake. Heavy rains were falling throughout this vast region. The water was being hoarded in the floodplains of Zambia and the forests of Angola, and in January the Sanyati river, which entered the Zambezi very near the new wall, suddenly came down like a cavalry charge. The river rose almost six metres in the next 24 hours and surged over the coffer dam. The largest digger truck, which had not been moved, disappeared instantly. Only in March, after much damage had been done and the project set back some months, did the river begin to subside. Such a flood should occur on average once every 1000 years.

Despite so dramatic a set-back, by December 1957 the Italians had completed a suspension bridge which towered high above the road crossing and, with the aid of substantial quantities of dynamite, the river was neatly channelled. It was expected that the wall would be completed at the end of the 1958 rains, but again freak weather was to prevent this.

Incredibly, and without warning, in January 1958 a flood such as could be expected to occur only once in every 10,000 years, swept down the river bed, wreaking havoc on all in its path. 16 million litres per second exploded over the suspension bridge which buckled and heaved. The north tower collapsed and the bridge rose clear of the water, bent like a gigantic bow. Its spine shattered in three places and the Zambezi carried away its battered remains with what appeared to be a roar of triumph. It certainly seemed that there was a malevolent force at work in the river, and some engineers swore that they had seen the monster leering at them from the lashing torrent.

'I felt at the time that we were confronted with a force far stronger than ourselves; the river was master', Baldassarini, Impresit's Chief Engineer, said at the time.

Only after the Zambezi had risen to a full 35 metres above its normal level did the flood start to subside. The tired engineers began their labour again and by December the Kariba Dam wall was complete. The extraordinary and hard-won triumph of man over

nature received little press attention or public reaction. Despite the total cost of 80 lives, the victors felt slightly ashamed of having brought about the humiliation of this mysterious and primeval river.

But the Tonga say that Nyaminyami is waiting, biding his time, and that one day he will exact a terrible revenge, a cataclysm that will reverberate around the world as the wall breaks and 174 billion tonnes of pent-up water is released. We hope they are wrong.

Operation Noah

The flooding of the Kariba Basin meant that countless animals faced the threat of drowning or starving on the islands that would remain above the water level. To alleviate this inevitable carnage, Operation Noah was set up by Rupert Fothergill, after whom an island has been named, Frank Junor, a young scientist, and Brian Hughes, an ex-fireman who could not swim.

Some argued that if an entire ecosystem was to be destroyed, so too should the animals that depended upon it. After all, government tsetse-control hunters had slaughtered more than 300,000 wild animals, the carriers of the fly, during the previous 12 years, and fewer larger mammals than that would drown in the flood; but humanitarian values prevailed and plans were made to translocate stranded animals to the mainland.

When the rains began in early December 1959, the lake filled six metres in the first 24 hours. Mice and snakes, driven from their holes by the rising water, clung onto rafts of debris floating downstream, together with countless insects, frogs and other unwilling sailors. Birds were taking full advantage of this surprise feast. Even the nocturnal owls were out, unable to resist the unexpected bonanza.

The rescue team set to work in their two small boats, feeling their way without any precedent to guide them. Their task was to save as many animals of all species as possible from the water and newly-formed islands and deliver them to the mainland. This was a mammoth task for an ill-equipped and under-financed team. It was only latterly, and largely too late to be of any real benefit that the plight of the animals captured the imagination of the world and help poured in.

Snakes were the first hazard. They would hang in the trees and drop among the rescuers as the boats passed underneath and a frantic scramble to catch the flailing reptiles would ensue. In this part of the world the common snakes, including the black mamba and Egyptian cobra, are often the most poisonous.

The lake rose rapidly. Islands became crowded and denuded of vegetation. At first the rescuers attempted to force the animals to swim by banging dustbin lids and hurling thunder-flashes among them. Antelope such as bushbuck escaped into the water and lay still, their noses just above the surface. When seized by human hands they struggled wildly, inflicting cuts and bruises with their thrashing hooves. Warthogs were responsible for the majority of casualties, causing frequent lacerations with their razor-sharp tusks.

The team found that the most efficient method of tackling an animal was to chase it into the water, and catch it by the tail before tying it to the boat and transporting it to safety. Baboons were uncooperative. Under pressure they dog-paddled to the mainland, but returned to their islands as soon as the men had gone. Waterbuck were observed swimming with their young clinging like jockeys to their backs. The adults helped each other. When one was tired, it would rest its head on another's back until it felt strong enough to assist the first in a similar manner. Impala, the most numerous of the antelope, refused to swim. Another idea was to put up lengths of netting 50 metres long and three metres high across the islands and drive the animals into them, once entangled they could be caught. But the team had limited success with this method as many animals died of shock.

So the rescuers began experimenting with tranquillizers and stimulants, and found this to be the most effective means of saving the larger mammals that refused to swim. Today's techniques in tranquillizing and moving animals owe much to Operation Noah.

Despite the feline distaste for water, it was found that lions and leopards could swim well when no other option presented itself. Some swam from island to island, dispatching the easy pickings they found there. Elephant and buffalo could swim to the mainland, but rhino remained stubborn to the last. One rhino cow became known as Greta Garbo, because of her truculence and reclusive habits. Refusing to budge from her island, despite repeated harrassment by the rescuers, she would chase them into the lake — nearly killing Fothergill one day. She did not otherwise venture near the water except to smash one of the boats. Sadly, Greta was abandoned to her fate. To ensure that this did not happen again, two experts in the field of immobilizing large animals were flown in. Several rhino were successfully darted and moved.

Animals under stress

Some interesting observations were made about animal behaviour when under this peculiar form of stress. Three cow elephants with calves refused to move from their island, knowing that their young ones would be incapable of swimming to the mainland. The calves were caught, but being too young to survive without their mothers had to be taken back. During further attempts to drive them off, one cow had to be shot in self-defence. A week later, the other two had gone. The mothers killed their babies before departing,

Larry Norton

rather than leaving them to drown or starve. The battered remains of the calves were found by the water's edge.

Even birds were trapped by the rising lake. The stronger, migratory species had no problems, but the smaller varieties were often unwilling to fly far from their customary surroundings. Many remained on their islands until too weak from hunger to make the long journey. They attempted to nest for months after their usual nesting time, desperate to pass on their genes before being overwhelmed by the catastrophe. One weaver built a double-storey residence, constructing a tunnel from his usual nest to another built above, to which he and his family could escape if the waters swamped the basement flat. Such behaviour had never before been recorded.

Monkeys were found to be natural swimmers. They would dive and swim breaststroke to depths of over five metres, their rescuers unable to pursue them. Porcupines were equipped with a life jacket in the form of quills, and antbears were almost as buoyant. Both swam slowly but confidently.

The team found that the hemp ropes they were using for binding the animals caused chafing sores and an appeal was sent out for nylon stockings. The response was overwhelming. A flood of stockings arrived from women all over the country. When the story reached the international news services, sufficient stockings for decades were received from the animal-loving British and American public. A BBC film added to the publicity and, with the aid of donations, the rescue operation was stepped up and more equipment purchased.

Most of the animals were placed on the Southern Rhodesian side, where two large game reserves had been set aside for them. In all over 6000 animals of 35 different species were rescued on the southern side, and some 2000 on the north bank when, in 1961, the project came to a close.

The maturing lake

Today, if you anchor your dinghy to one of the dead trees along the shoreline and cast a hook and worm among the weeds, you might be lucky enough to pull in a couple of lively bream, a *Tilapia* species. Filleted and fried with lemon juice, they make a delicious dinner aboard your houseboat as you sip beer and watch the buffalo on the bank and the red sun dip behind the trees. But 20 years ago you would probably still be out fishing, the dinghy groaning under the weight of your catch.

It was foreseen that the formation of the lake would create a few ecological hiccups but not how they would manifest themselves. The unprecedented appearance of a great expanse of calm water in this fecund environment would offer fresh opportunities for colonization by plants and fish normally unable to compete in the fast-flowing current.

Before the wall sealed it off, the character of the river through the Kariba Basin had changed dramatically over the course of each year. During the rains, floodwaters surged over the banks and inundated surrounding low-lying lands, providing increased living space and food for the fish. They spawned prolifically. In the dry season the river shrank to a fraction of its former size and large numbers of fingerlings were confined to a much smaller area, with fewer food resources and less cover. They were then at the mercy of the predatory tigerfish (*Hydrocynus vittatus*) and the fish population which had bred during the rains was rapidly depleted. A survey conducted in this part of the river before the lake rose, revealed the presence of only 26 fish species, less than a third of which were small varieties; the tigerfish dominated the river. The damming of Kariba dramatically changed these conditions. As the waters rose, vegetation and rotting animal matter contributed to a sudden increase in available nutrients and an explosive growth of algae and plankton. The closure of the wall coincided with the breeding season of most species. There was suddenly more food and cover available and the fish population mushroomed. But when gradually the lake stabilized and the nutrient value diminished, so too did the extraordinary fish density. The food web is now more equitably balanced.

Unfortunately an aquatic fern (*Salvinia auriculata*), probably of South or Central American origins, also found the new conditions to its liking. By May 1960 it covered about 20 percent of the lake's surface. Ecologists despaired and it was feared that the fern might choke the entire lake.

However, in 1962 the weed began to decline. This was due in part to the introduction by National Parks of a South American grasshopper (*paulina*), which ate the prolific plant with relish. But as with the fish, the major cause of the decline of the Kariba weed was probably the decreasing fertility of the water, and it is now present only in the creeks and quiet backwaters of the lake.

Kapenta fishing

The sardines from Lake Tanganyika were introduced to Kariba as an experiment to boost the potential of commercial fishing. There was an unexploited niche in the food web of the new lake in that the resident species were utilizing the shoreline and did not venture into open waters. It was hoped that the plankton-eating sardine would fill this ecological vacuum. Such introductions are often fraught with difficulties, but the sardine, known locally as kapenta, has been an unprecedented success. Although they do not grow as large as their brothers nearer the equator, reaching only about five centimetres in length, they thrive in sufficient numbers to make commercial fishing a lucrative industry, and fulfil a much-needed protein requirement.

At dusk the kapenta rigs set off across the lake from their various harbours like a line of dung beetles on a pane of glass, to anchor on the open waters and began the evening's fishing. Kapenta are attracted to light and are caught with huge round gill nets lowered from pontoons into the water. An electric bulb suspended above the net attracts the sardines, which are trapped in the mesh as it is hauled to the surface.

Today the lake has become a kind of Zimbabwean riviera. Hotels have sprung up and visitors enjoy watersports such as water-skiing and wind-surfing. The predatory tigerfish, one of Africa's finest fighters, equipped with razor-sharp teeth and a ferocious temperament, provides challenging sport for anglers. In the evenings, the roulette wheel and blackjack table offer entertainment of a different sort. Yet the lake as a whole remains strangely unspoilt and undeveloped.

In Kariba township itself the wild is never far away and elephant often wander among the houses at night, raiding vegetable gardens. Leopards have taken domestic cats and dogs within the fences of urban gardens. Most of the southern shoreline is designated as National Park and hunting areas and far from ruining the ecosystem, the lake has in many ways enhanced the natural beauty of the area. Urbanization has only encroached on a minute proportion of the available landspace, and on the Zambian side there has been virtually no development at all. Perhaps Nyaminyami has at last come to terms with his new role as god of the lake, and finds it not uncomfortable.

Larry Norton.

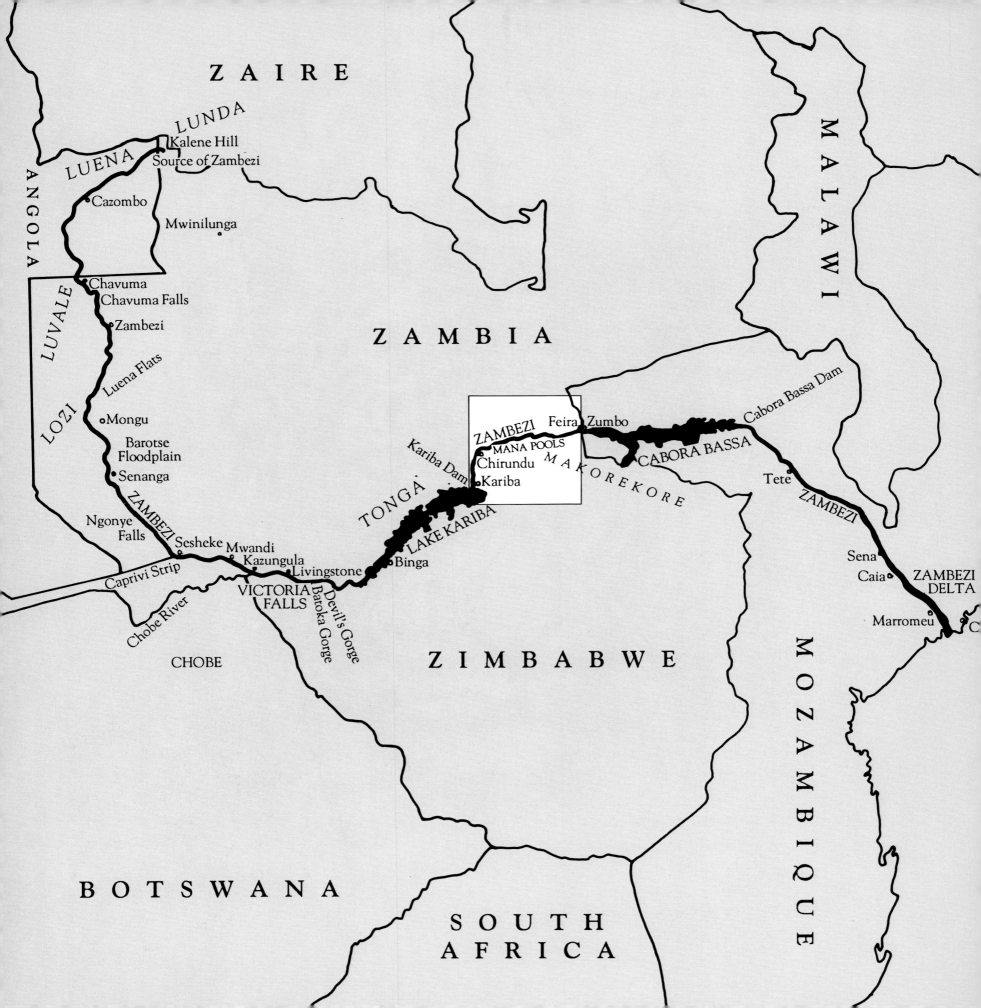

ZAIRE

LUNDA

Kalene Hill
Source of Zambezi

LUENA

ANGOLA

Cazombo

Mwinilunga

ZAMBIA

LUVALE

Chavuma
Chavuma Falls

Zambezi

Luena Flats

LOZI

Mongu

Barotse
Floodplain

Senanga

ZAMBEZI

Ngonye
Falls

Sesheke
Mwandi
Kazungula
Caprivi Strip
Livingstone

VICTORIA
FALLS

Devil's Gorge
Batoka Gorge

Chobe River

CHOBE

Kariba Dam

TONGA

Binga

LAKE KARIBA

ZAMBEZI
MANA POOLS
Chirundu
Kariba

Feira Zumbo

MAKOREKORE

CABORA BASSA

Cabora Bassa Dam

Tete

ZAMBEZI

Sena
Caia

ZAMBEZI
DELTA

Marromeu

C

MALAWI

MOZAMBIQUE

ZIMBABWE

BOTSWANA

SOUTH
AFRICA

MIDDLE ZAMBEZI VALLEY

piercing whistle echoed across the gorge, followed by yells and high-pitched barking. We scrambled out from under our mosquito net, scanning the rugged terrain on the other side of the river. A shaft of sunlight slipped over the hills, bathing the valley in early morning warmth. Another whistle, more barking. At the top of the ridge stood a young kudu cow. She hesitated momentarily before plunging down the wooded slope, the dogs on her heels. She leapt clear of the tree-line and stopped on the bank, flanks heaving, her neck bathed in sweat. Her nose quivered as she stared into the water. An ear flicked back, listening for the approaching howls. She looked behind her. The dogs were closer, yapping and baying as they sprang from rock to rock. Their handler shouted encouragement as he chased after them, spear in hand. Suddenly she jumped, disappearing in the swirling current. Her head bobbed to the surface and, struggling wildly, she forced her way across and clambered exhausted onto the opposite bank. She gazed back at the barking dogs, then turned away and started browsing.

Kariba Gorge

It was New Year's day. We were canoeing through the Kariba Gorge and had camped on a sandy spit on the Zimbabwean bank. Before the dam was built a treacherous whirlpool had marked the entrance to the gorge. We drifted gently downstream, the sultry silence broken by the occasional splash of eddies forming and disappearing, and the incessant call of emerald-spotted doves:

My mother is dead,
my father is dead.
All my relatives are dead
and my heart goes dum-dum-dum.

Bare quartzite boulders line the banks. Shaped and eroded by the current, they resemble a gallery of modern sculpture. Beyond these, sheer rock faces rise to the tree-line. The heavily wooded foothills give way to precipitous peaks, towering above the water.

For 30 kilometres the river winds its way through the heavily dissected, mountainous terrain of the Zambezi escarpment which borders most of the valley from the lake to the Mozambique border. The gorge was created by downfaulting of the Karoo sediments between the stable, granite cratons forming the Zimbabwean and Zambian plateaux. The process was further enhanced by the upwarping, folding and thrusting of the craton edges and the erosion of numerous tributaries. The rocks that line the gorge date back some 2500 million years.

Two Augur buzzards wheeled overhead and a dassie (or rock rabbit) disappeared into the safety of a rock crevice. A large crocodile, mouth agape, dozed on the bank. He slid silently into the water as we approached, eyes and nostrils cutting the surface.

The crocodile is a living archesaur, unchanged in 70 million years. It has suffered the depredations of man in the last century, in some areas to extinction. In Zimbabwe, however, crocodile populations are now stable and healthy. This recovery has been due to protection legislated by government, preventing hunting or capture except on special licence. Commercial crocodile farms collect eggs from captive females and from the wild and incubate and hatch them. The young crocodiles are harvested at three years of age and the skins sold to the European market, realizing over US$1,000,000 annually in foreign exchange. The crocodile farms are obliged to return five percent of the wild egg hatchlings to the rivers, a far higher proportion than the 0.2 percent that would normally survive out in the wild.

The monotonous *Piet-my-vrow, piet-my-vrow*, of red-chested cuckoos echoed through the hills, interrupted by the sporadic honking of purple louries and the haunting cry of a soaring fish eagle as we continued downstream.

The valley floor

The gorge ends abruptly, giving way to the undulating woodland of the Zambezi Valley. This vast downfaulted trough covers some 8000 square kilometres between the Kariba and Mupata Gorges. Here the river meanders over its own alluvium, changing its course as the channels silt up and reopen between shifting sandbars. On the Zimbabwean side the valley forms the major part of the middle Zambezi wilderness complex, made up of three hunting areas and Mana Pools National Park, extending from Kariba wall to the Mozambique border. The Zambian bank is sparsely inhabited as far as the Lower Zambezi National Park, and was declared a protected area in 1973.

The valley floor consists of a series of terraces of changing soil types and vegetation, stretching from the base of the escarpments to the water's edge. The highest of these supports the 'jesse'— dense, inhospitable, deciduous forest where tsetse flies are rampant and water scarce. This opens into mopane woodland, broken by stretches of grassland and dotted with alkaline pans. Nearer the river the *Acacia albida* becomes the dominant tree of the flood-plain and river banks, and is interspersed with stands of Natal mahogany, figs, sausage trees and numerous other species.

The seasons

In November billowing storm clouds break and the rains come, filling the waterholes and flooding the sand rivers. The animals leave the floodplain and disappear into the revitalized jesse . The rains end abrubtly and the relentless sun sucks the valley dry. The smaller pools evaporate rapidly, leaving depressions of cracked, baked clay. Others form mud baths, seething with catfish or barbel flopping around in the remaining moisture. Marabou storks gather like crusty old bank managers to exploit the writhing protein source. The bush turns brown and a dusty haze hangs over the trees. The animals start their migration back to the perennial waters of the Zambezi where the *Acacia albida* is at the peak of its inverted cycle, fruiting in massive quantities. A single tree may bear 80 kilogrammes of pods a

year, with a crude protein content of around 15 percent. The sausage tree drops its mass of maroon and yellow flowers, welcome delicacies for the baboons. Natal mahogany trees are pruned to a neat inverted table-top by kudu, impala and eland, which browse the bitter green leaves. Finally the springs and pools on the escarpment run dry and herds of buffalo and elephant appear overnight. It is a time of plenty for the predators. The savage heat of October burns fiercely into November, and the few clouds that collect to taunt the parched landscape drift slowly away. At last the rains come; the bush bursts into verdant life and the cycle is completed once more.

We camped in the shade of a Natal mahogany, rising at first light for a long walk. Three years of drought had taken their toll. Signs of hardship mingled with the green succulence of good rains. In many places the grass had not revived and the red earth had been trampled into a giant dust bowl. Buffalo carcases, skeletons intact and the skins bleached and hardened by the sun, were scattered throughout the bush. Lions and other predators had not been able to keep up with the endless meat supply. Drought is nature's great selector and only the strongest survive. In the Zambezi Valley it is not the lack of water that kills, but scarcity of food.

The tsetse fly

The tsetse fly, the scourge of Africa, has probably been the greatest single factor in preventing settlement and destruction of this unique ecosystem. In Zambia and Zimbabwe most development has taken place on the central plateaux, where the fly has been eradicated and where soils are richer and water supplies permanent. The tsetse-infested area of the middle Zambezi Valley has been left for the most part to the animals and the few peasant farmers whose lifestyle is adapted to the harsh environment and the absence of livestock.

Two of the seven species of this blood-feeding fly occur along the Zambezi, the most prevalent being *Glossina morsitans*. The tsetse acts as host for trypanosomes, blood parasites which cause 'sleeping sickness' in humans and a fatal disease in livestock, *nagana*.

A major challenge to doctors and scientists, millions have been spent on tsetse eradication and its former range has been greatly reduced. Livingstone outlined the first possible solution to the problem in 1865: 'The destruction of all game by the advance of civilization is the only chance of getting rid of the tsetse.'

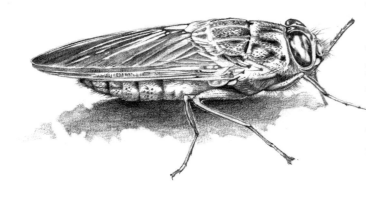

Sadly this theory of the creation of an animal desert was encouraged by the rinderpest epidemic of 1895/96, which killed thousands of animals and dramatically diminished the fly belt.

In 1900 the tsetse was threatening cattle ranches in Southern Rhodesia and an entomologist was employed to assess the situation. In 1919 intensive hunting began, with the aim of eliminating all large wild vertebrates in areas where the fly was most prevalent. Early operations were small-scale and somewhat disorganized, but in 1933 the exercise was intensified. African hunters were employed and using old military 0.303 rifles, they hunted 25 days a month. Their wages were low and they supplemented their incomes by selling meat from the culls.

In 1954 a commission was set up to develop a method of tsetse control less embarrassing than mass animal destruction. A buffer zone consisting of a 16-kilometre wide, game-free corridor, was fenced along the edge of the valley. In 1960 hunting ceased. Over 650,000 animals from 36 different species had been shot and still the tsetse remained. The operation was a resounding failure.

The buffer zone could not contain the fly and inevitably insecticides became the centre of the tsetse eradication programme and DDT spraying began in 1968. Cheap and easy to apply, it became the mainstay of control. DDT is a chlorinated hydrocarbon which, although highly effective as an insecticide, has a cumulative effect in vertebrate body tissues. Banned from general use in Europe and North America, and from agricultural use in Zimbabwe, it may still be applied for 'scientific purposes', hence its continued use in tsetse control.

High levels of DDE, a metabolite of DDT, have been found in crocodile eggs in Lake Kariba. Despite this the EEC continues to finance spraying programmes and in 1988, 2000 square kilometres were covered with some 100 tonnes of chemical on the shores of Lake Kariba. Although in a token gesture to conservation the EEC has sponsored a study of the effects of DDT on bird, fish and bat populations in contaminated areas, it continues to poison the region.

Experiments with baited tsetse traps began in the early 1970s and continue to be used today. The fly is attracted by dark moving bodies and animal odour. Black, kite-like traps coated in insecticide and containing a pouch of a substance releasing ox-odour are used. Each trap is effective over an area of one square kilometre. They have been placed at regular intervals through much of the valley and have been most successful.

But as Zimbabwe fights the tsetse, economic depression and war have virtually stopped all control measures in Zambia and Mozambique. Zimbabwe is an island in a vast fly zone and eradication cannot be achieved in isolation. Escalating costs may force a change in policy — to limit the tsetse rather than destroy it. In this case the Zambezi Valley may still be saved for its wildlife heritage, but it is questionable why the EEC and other aid-donating organizations fund resettlement ventures and subsidize beef production in habitats best suited to wildlife, while there are beef surpluses in most of Europe and America. Africa's

wildlife is a unique natural resource which, if properly utilized, could become enormously profitable.

Chirundu village

On the islands and sandbars yellow-billed storks, spoonbills and Egyptian geese fed in the shallows. A pair of painted snipe skulked in the weeds. African jacanas (*Actophiloruis africana*) darted busily across the reed mats, snatching at insects.

We were nearing Chirundu, a village named after a hill, where a chief once built his hut in the hope of finding a cool breeze in the oppressive heat of the valley. In 1939 the Otto Beit Bridge was completed across the river, linking the capitals of Northern and Southern Rhodesia, and Chirundu became a border post.

In 1948 this tiny village emerged as the centre of a sugar-growing scheme. 700 hectares of cane were planted, irrigated by the Zambezi, and by 1963 the estates employed 4000 people and boasted electricity, an excellent sewage system, a school, a cinema and the beginnings of a hospital. Suddenly world sugar prices collapsed. Today the estate is part of the Urungwe Safari Area, comprising 300,000 hectares of protected wilderness between the escarpment and the river from Kariba to Mana Pools National Park.

Chirundu remains a scruffy border post. As the trucks lie waiting for clearance on the Zimbabwean side they are carefully inspected by the 'border patrol', a raggle-taggle troop of baboons who manage to pry their way into any edible cargo and spend most of the day lounging in the shadows of the pantechnicons. Elephant wander through the village, sucking the hotel swimming pool dry and regularly cracking its bottom as they slide in for a wallow. Anglers leave their city jobs and dash up on Friday afternoons to camp on the river's edge for a weekend of fishing. Their fires glow between the trees as they consume cold lager and bait their night-lines with ox-heart or blue soap in the hope of catching vundu, a giant catfish which may reach 50 kilogrammes in weight. But the main attraction is the tigerfish, pound for pound the most ferocious freshwater fighter in the world. Its Latin name, *Hydrocynus forskahlii*, 'water dog', is an apt description for this voracious predator which can swallow whole fish of up to 40 percent of its own weight.

The black rhinoceros

Selous[1] described them as the most common of the big game but today, only 100 years later, the hook-lipped or black rhinoceros is facing extinction. The uses of rhino horn for the handles of the Yemenese dagger, *djambia*, and as an aphrodisiac in India have been well documented, but the greatest demand today comes from China and Japan. Both

1. **Courtney Frederick Selous** — b. 1851, London. Hunter and naturalist, he visited the Zambezi on several occasions in 1880, 1882 and 1888.

countries use the horn in traditional medicine for the curing of fever, colds, allergies and a host of minor ailments. In fact boiled keratin has no known medicinal properties and most of the powder sold is an imitation product. Indeed, more so-called rhino horn is sold daily than could possibly be produced from the dwindling rhino populations.

Asian horn has always been deemed superior to African, but the sharp decline in Asian rhinoceros populations in the late 19th century led to the increased use of the African species. In 1960 there was estimated to be one million black rhinos in Africa. Today there are probably less than 3500. Demand for horn seems insatiable and the rhinos are now facing the greatest threat to their existence since the North Yemenese boom in trade during the early 1970s. Despite a government ban on all trade in rhino products in 1985, Taiwan has become the world's largest entrepot for the horn. The law has never been enforced and traders are offering up to US$40,000 per kilogramme of horn. They continue to increase their stocks, investing in the rhino's probable extinction.

The middle Zambezi Valley is one of the last strongholds of these prehistoric creatures. Zimbabwe's rhinoceros population was relatively stable until 1983. Up to that time markets were supplied with horn poached from countries to the north, where badly administered National Parks and government corruption made the rhinoceros an easy target. Inevitably demand outstripped supply and, with dwindling or extinct populations in these countries, greedy eyes focused on Zimbabwe. Zambian peasants, whose yearly income could barely buy a blanket let alone feed a family, were easily cajoled into providing convenient bases for poaching operations.

Larry Norton. 89

'Save the Rhino'

The Zimbabweans responded aggressively. Operation Stronghold became the code name for the rhino protection exercise which continues today. Army and National Parks patrols try to track and capture poachers before they can cause any damage. Unfortunately they are often too late. Over 500 carcases have been recovered in the last few years, probably half the number of rhinos actually killed.

Funded by conservation organizations from all over the world and the concerned public, the 'Save the Rhino' campaign was launched with the objective of moving rhinos from the Valley and creating viable breeding populations in protected areas around Zimbabwe. The problems facing such an exercise are immense. The hook-lipped rhinoceros is a solitary creature which browses and rests in dense cover. The increase in poaching has triggered its survival instinct and the animals are wary and nervous, hiding by day and moving to water at night. The only efficient method of locating them is from the air and then radioing sightings to a darting team on the ground.

A drug known as M99, combined with a tranquillizer, is injected by means of a six-centimetre dart fired from a bored-out 0.458 rifle. The rhino runs off as the dart penetrates its hide and must be carefully tracked until the drug takes effect.

Transportation is a major problem. The animals stand in heavy crates which open at both ends. The bumping and jolting over rough roads to the initial holding *bomas* (stalls), followed by a long journey to their new homes, puts the animals under considerable stress and there have been several casualties. Moving a rhino is costly and most of the operations have been hampered by unreliable vehicles and inadequate manpower. In spite of the frustrations, the dedication of the capture teams has never wavered. By the end of 1988, 300 rhinos had been moved to protected areas.

Authorities estimate the number of rhino remaining in the valley at anywhere between 200 and 800 individuals. Carcases are still found almost daily, and contacts with poachers are frequent. In 1988 the WWF — World Wide Fund for Nature donated the use of a helicopter to Operation Stronghold to good effect. Rhino kills fell to their lowest levels since 1985, although these figures have to be qualified against the increasing difficulty of locating them. Sadly Zimbabwean National Parks have since failed to come up with an effective rhino conservation policy and the WWF has now withdrawn the helicopter.

In the Valley Zimbabwe is losing the 'rhino war', for a war is what it has become. To protect the *in-situ* populations effectively, a scout force five times the current size and a budget double the entire National Parks annual grant would be needed. Every year since independence has seen a reduction in treasury funds for National Parks. Unless there is a

radical change in policy, it seems unlikely that the rhino protection demands will be fulfilled.

Conservationists have been working on the problem for 20 years, but they seem as far from success now as they were at the start. Africa's poverty is at the heart of the problem. In most countries on the continent, the bulk of the population is made up of peasant farmers, earning an average of US$2 a month. Businessmen and government officials form the bridge between Africa and the developed world. They buy the horn for what seems a fortune to the African supplier and sell to the end users at huge profits. Their greed and the ever-growing demand fan the flames. Whether or not the rhino becomes extinct hinges entirely on the implementation of an effective ban on the trade in rhino horn or the production of an 'authentic' synthetic.

Zimbabwe's hope in this desolate scene is that the translocated animals will form a successful breeding population, and progress reports are encouraging. Birth and death rates are now about equal, but most encouraging of all is that there has been a marked change in attitude towards environmental problems in the developed world in recent years. It is to be hoped that this new approach will be adopted by Africa and the East while there is still time to preserve the species.

The nature of the beast

Five years ago we saw rhino daily in Mana Pools, often at most inconvenient moments. One chilly May morning we watched three cheetahs hunting impala. Two charged from the right of our vehicle, missing their quarry, but the third brought down a young doe. She disembowelled the carcass and then sat over it, calling the others with high-pitched, bird-like chirps. 15 minutes later they reappeared and dragged the impala to the safety of a dense bush. The timid cheetah is often chased off its kill by lions or hyenas. The three bolted their meal and we were able to edge in closer. Suddenly, heralded by a violent crashing in a nearby thicket, a rhino thundered towards us and skidded to a halt a few metres away. The cheetahs crouched, waiting to run. The rhino grunted, swivelled on his hind legs and trotted off. Somewhat shaken, we turned back to the kill.

The black rhinoceros has managed to acquire a reputation for being excessively dangerous, but although it can be irascible and unpredictable we could find no reports or record of human fatalities brought about by rhino attacks.

Mana Pools

Mana Pools, proclaimed a protected area in 1963, achieved National Park status under the Parks and Wildlife Act 1975. The Park and the adjoining Sapi and Chewore Safari Areas have recently been declared a World Heritage Site by UNESCO, one of the highest accolades in international conservation.

The area has developed as the Zambezi has shifted northwards over thousands of years, leaving alluvial terraces three kilometres wide and traversed by its abandoned river channels. Some of these contain deep pools, which hold water all year round. The word *mana* means four, describing the four largest perennial pools. The riparian plain supports vast stretches of acacia and mixed woodland. On the Zambian bank the valley terracing has been virtually obliterated by the escarpment, which rises close to the northern banks of the Zambezi and provides a magnificent backdrop to the river.

The bushmen say that Gawe, the great spirit, gave every species of animal a tree, except the hyena.

'Stop stealing and be good and I will give you a tree,' commanded the spirit. But the hyena was angry and refused to change his ways. The spirit said, 'Here, this tiny baobab plant is the last. You may have it. The hyena was furious, and taking the seedling, planted it upside down.

Ecologists have generally assumed that the Zambezi flooded annually before Kariba was built, inundating and recharging the fertility of the riverine habitat. Chief Dandawa's people, who lived here before the dam was built, deny this. They say the Zambezi flooded twice a year. *Gumbura*, the 'dirty' flood came in February and was caused by local runoff after the rains. *Murorwe*, the 'clean' water from the catchment area of the upper Zambezi, came later and lasted about two weeks. On only four occasions did the water rise enough to inundate the terraces — in 1916, 1934 and during the infamous 1957 and 1958 floods.

So the main reason for the vegetation being less dense than previously remembered is probably due to increasing animal pressure, especially elephant. At the turn of the century there were about 5000 elephants in Zimbabwe. They were scarce in the valley, probably because of overhunting, but as commercial farms encroached on their habitats in the northern highveld, they gradually moved down the escarpment. Protection by National Parks and rapid breeding rates have resulted in a tenfold increase in the overall population. There are an estimated 12,000 in the middle Zambezi Valley. As a result, the trees, especially the *Acacia albida*, do not get a chance to mature.

The mythical baobab

The baobab (*Adansonia digitata*) has also suffered. They may live for several thousand years, and are a focus of native folk-lore and spiritualism, especially among the valley tribes. The white flowers are said to be inhabited by spirits and myth has it that anyone who plucks a bloom will be devoured by lions before the year is out. The young leaves are used as a vegetable, the fruit pods as gourds, and the cream of tartare from the flesh of the fruits as a thirst quencher. The bark may be softened and woven into mats and rope and as the vast trunks often become hollow, they have over the years been used as outhouses, prisons and store-rooms. It is a common belief that old trees are consumed by fire and there are a few reports of spontaneous combustion. However death is usually brought by a virus which causes the tree to collapse in a mound of pulp. Elephants hasten this progress, especially in drought years when the baobab fibre forms an important source of nutrition for these giant pachyderms.

The elephant problem

Culling and trophy hunting have been used to control elephant populations in both Zambia and Zimbabwe and although the ethics of the former have been debated for years, it remains the only effective method of preventing dramatic, large-scale destruction of vegetation.

In economic terms, culling provides ivory and hide which are a valuable source of foreign exchange and are vital to the thriving curio industries. With increasing demands on land and natural resources, preservation of wildlife, and of the elephant in particular, must be made financially viable.

But the systematic slaughter of these gentle giants, however scientifically and efficiently performed, is naturally abhorrent. We were in Mana Pools during two culling operations and observed that the elephants vanished into the jesse before the first shots had been fired, gradually reappearing when the exercise was over. The complexity of elephant communication, like that of the whale, is beginning to come to light. The most common vocalization is the so called 'tummy rumble', emanating from the vocal cords. Recent research indicates that it may also communicate by infrasonic sounds produced in the nasal passages on the animal's forehead, detectable by other elephants over a distance of several kilometres.

Larry Norton '89

The CITES ban on trade in elephant products is a desperate but necessary attempt to save the virtually extinct populations in many African countries where the national parks systems have collapsed. These measures will certainly effect the economics of culling in Zimbabwe which in turn will limit the extent of such operations. The decrease in revenue and the attendant ecological problems need to be carefully weighed against the ever decreasing funds granted annually by the Zimbabwean government to the upkeep of her parks. Without adequate financial backing, management levels in these wildlife areas will gradually collapse and the elephant will come under severe poaching pressure. If, unlike the theoretical ban on the trade in rhino horn, the CITES ban is effectively implemented, it could prove vital to the prevention of the future mass destruction of Zimbabwe's elephants. But it is depressingly difficult to envisage a secure method of preventing inevitable corruption from undermining such a decree.

Rare moments

Mana Pools is one of the few game reserves in Africa where visitors are free to walk and do so at their own risk. The experiment has been a success and there have been surprisingly few accidents. Most of the wildlife pictures in this book were taken here. The intimate contact with animals afforded by hours of quiet observation is thrilling, if sometimes a little nerve-wracking.

Wildlife photography depends largely on luck and persistence. Two years ago we heard that a male and female leopard had been seen together near our camp. These cats are normally solitary and so we presumed they were mating. At first light the following morning we spent two hours searching for them and had almost given up hope when we spotted a camouflaged leg and a white-tipped tail dangling from an acacia. We sat, not daring to take our eyes off the tree in case the elusive cat dis- appeared. There was a rustle in the grass and the female appeared, settling down no more than 30 metres away. An hour later she slunk away and climbed up to join her mate. She rubbed herself against him, purring loudly, but he turned his back and resumed his siesta.

Eight hours later, just as the light was beginning to fade, the male sat up, stretched and started to groom himself. His lady strolled out from behind a bush and he leapt to the ground. She brushed herself seductively against him and they disappeared into the vetiveria grass. We sat listening helplessly to the growls that accompanied their mating. The sun was disappearing fast when, without warning, the pair padded into a small clearing. The male stood staring at us for a few minutes, then lay down. The female swayed towards him and he mounted her, never taking his eyes off us. Three, four seconds and it was over. Their coats blended into the grass as they slipped away.

The warthog (njiri) *had enormous tusks, so big he could barely lift them off the ground. The elephant* (nzou) *had tiny, inward curling tusks and was very jealous of the warthog. The pangolin*[1] (haka) *was worried for his friend* njiri *and warned him that the elephant was planning a trick, but the kindly warthog took no notice so it happened one day the elephant came to him.*

'Dear njiri, *your tusks are so fine and mine are so small, could I borrow yours for a day?'*

'Of course nzou. *Here.' They swopped tusks and the elephant walked off laughing,*

'Stupid njiri, *did you really believe I would return them? You're too ugly for these fine tusks.' The warthog rushed off and told the pangolin.*

'Don't worry, dear njiri. Nzou *will be hunted forever for those tusks. He will have no home where he can hide. But you, dear friend, can use my burrow as your home.'*

1. **Pangolin** — a scaly ant-eater.

The predator-prey relationship is harsh and uncompromising and the young, weak or injured are the usual targets, but we occasionally witnessed incidents that added a gentle touch to this tough environment. At dawn one morning we found a dead baboon lying in the grass, her tiny infant clinging to her body, crying piteously and trying to suckle. The mother had been killed by a leopard which had then been chased off by the furious troop. We waited quietly. Half an hour later, a female baboon came down from the trees and started to comfort and groom the orphan. She was joined by another female. They passed the baby back and forwards between them. The second female was lactating and the baby eventually started to suckle. A few minutes later the adopted infant was carried back to the troop.

Abundant bird life

Birdlife in the valley is spectacular. During the rains woodland kingfishers sing from the trees, their beautiful chants mingling with the raucous clamouring of ducks and waders. Emerald-spotted, turtle and laughing doves murmur in the background. Young fish eagles, unable to compete for prime territories, fight for supremacy over the tiniest pans. In October, thousands of carmine bee-eaters nest in holes in the river banks. The Zambezi constantly erodes the sandy banks, a process undoubtedly accelerated by the relatively constant water levels maintained by Lake Kariba. Large stretches break off and crash into the water, leaving steep sand cliffs, perfect breeding sites for the bee-eaters. The sky fills with flashes of brilliant pink as the birds leave their holes, twisting and turning like spitfires as they snatch passing insects from the air.

As the river flows east into the Sapi and Chewore Safari Areas, its channel moves gradually south towards the Zimbabwean escarpment and the hills on the Zambian side recede into the distance. Ever present is the chatter of the ground hornbills:

'How much is that hat?'
'Two and six, two and six',
'It's too much, it's too much,
one and three, one and three',
'Two shillings, two shillings',
'I'll take it, I'll take it,
and wear it on Sunday.'

It was first light and as we sat up we startled a family of warthogs emerging sleepily from their hole nearby. Like a platoon on the parade square, the little family wheeled in unison and trotted smartly away, tails erect. We were camped at the mouth of the Chewore river, on the border of one of the wildest safari areas in Zimbabwe. Once the home of Chief

Chimombe and his people, the Va-Sori, the area is now controlled by National Parks. Apart from a few canoeists passing through, the only people to visit this remote corner of the valley are trophy hunters.

Primitive man hunted out of necessity and the hunting instinct, once vital to the preservation of the race, has never been totally eradicated. It is an expensive business and is today recognized as an important source of foreign currency since, if properly managed, it is extremely profitable.

Early inhabitants

Bushmen were the earliest inhabitants of the Zambezi Valley. They were gradually displaced around the middle of the 15th century by the Va-Mbara, Bantu-speaking people from Zambia. They settled in small, scattered communities in inaccessible parts of the valley. They were miners and metal workers and their skills allowed them to coexist with the powerful Makorekore, who were the 'rulers of the land'. They traded gold and metal objects such as spears, hoes and axes, with the Makorekore, who in turn sold these to the Portuguese.

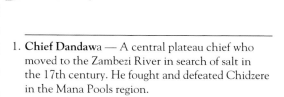

The Makorekore were an offshoot of the Karanga, the people responsible for the construction of Great Zimbabwe, which are the ruins found near Masvingo in the south of the country. In 1400 AD, led by the legendary Mutota, they moved north, seeking control of trading routes with the Arabs on the coast. They were also drawn by reports of abundant natural salt in the Zambezi Valley. They settled on the escarpment, some moving as far as Tete. The local inhabitants nick- named them *makorekore*, 'like a swarm of locusts', and the ruler of this new state took the dynastic title *mwene mutapa*, 'master pillager'.

As the Portuguese traders became more powerful and clashes with the reigning *mwene mutapa* more frequent, so the market for Va-Mbara products fell away. These industrious people found they were no longer safe, and those who could fled back across the Zambezi.

In the 17th century there was a second Va-Mbara migration. Led by Chief Chidzere, they settled on the south bank of the Zambezi between Chirundu and the Sapi river, relying on shifting riverine cultivation and hunting. Inevitably, they came into conflict with Chief Dandawa[1] who was moving into the valley from the Zimbabwean plateau. He implored Chidzere to share the land. Chidzere refused and was defeated in the ensuing battle. Most of his followers fled across the Zambezi and folklore has it that when Chidzere died he turned into a giant baobab. His sister, Changamuchire, refused to flee and died also. It is said that her spirit was trapped in a smooth stone bearing four holes. The stone moves and apparently visits Mana Pools to drink and bath, and whenever it travels through

1. **Chief Dandaw**a — A central plateau chief who moved to the Zambezi River in search of salt in the 17th century. He fought and defeated Chidzere in the Mana Pools region.

Chief Nyamapfeka, my ancestor, made war on Chimombe.

They had taken our land. But when our warriors got there, Chimombe made a mist so they could not see. Our chief was very angry and decided to trick Chimombe. He sent his daughter, Semwa, to visit. She was very beautiful and Chimombe decided to marry her. The night of the wedding, Semwa cut the chief's throat while he slept. The hut filled with blood and it ran from the door. It flowed on, making the Musikoto river. There was darkness and drought. Then there were floods. At last we sent an offering of beads, black cloth and beer to Chimombe's spirit. The flood went down.

Chimombe's body floated down the blood river. At last it came to rest in a circle of muchichiri trees where it disappeared. In its place rose up the Iron God. The people took the god and put it in a house. It is looked after by Chief Chundu. We Makorekore cannot see it or we will become blind.

Even the Matabele could not fight the Iron God. An impi[1] stole him one day. The tribe took the god up the river in canoes, but every time they stopped, a man was eaten by a lion. They were so frightened they threw the god into the river, but he jumped back out onto the sand. They tried to drown him again, but again he appeared on the bank. Eventually they all ran away so Chimombe went back home. The Matabele never came again.

---

1. **Impi** — Matabele war party

the valley is accompanied by a roaring wind. While the Va-Mbara were settling on the south bank of the river a group known as the Va-Sori, led by Chief Chimombe, were making their homes near the Chewore river.

As the river meanders on, its terraces are replaced by low hills and the channel narrows. The Chewore mountains rise dark against the sky as the river enters the Mupata Gorge. The steep, heavily forested terrain bordering the gorge does not deter the animals and is a haven for birds of prey. Brown-necked parrots screech high in the air as they flap furiously against the wind. The rocky islands in midstream provide perfect hideouts for the shy, nocturnal white-backed night heron. We found a pair with three chicks and, as we slid forward quietly and peered over the ledge, the nervous adults sensed our presence. They stared at us for a few minutes with their huge eyes and then flew off, leaving the downy chicks to camouflage themselves as best they could.

The environmental struggle

The rapidly increasing urban population in Zimbabwe has fuelled a demand for additional power supplies. The search for a new dam site on which to set up a hydro-electric scheme focused attention on the Mupata gorge. A dam built here would flood most of the valley, including Mana Pools and would destroy the remaining natural stretches of the Zambezi between Kariba and Cabora Bassa. Fortunately the geology of the gorge is not entirely suitable and a better site has been surveyed in the Batoka Gorge which would be ecologically less damaging and geologically more stable. Thus the valley has earned a temporary reprieve.

But another environmental war is beginning. A large oil company is planning a multi-million dollar oil exploration venture in the valley. The project may necessitate the cutting of traces five metres wide at 15-kilometre intervals throughout the valley, and setting up operational camps and equipment bases. Environmental impact studies have not been completed. Much of the area in question is a world heritage site and any exploration is in direct conflict with the conservation responsibilities required for such an area. The oil company argues that they will create very little permanent damage, but the devastation caused by a similar project in the Luangwa Valley provides evidence to the contrary.

We moved on to Kanyemba, a tiny outpost on the border of Zambia, Zimbabwe and Mozambique. It is named after the notorious Chief Kanyemba or *Sergento Mor* (Sergeant Death) as he was known. This man was an African slaver who had an army of 9000 men to control the Zambezi north bank during the lawless years of the 19th century.

Today Kanyemba is a small administrative post serving the Dande communal lands. The District Assistant's camp, a chain of cottages overlooking the river, stands derelict and overgrown. The police station faces downstream to the confluence of the Luangwa river. On the Zambian bank is a squalid little village called Feira which has little importance today but which, at the turn of the century, was an administrative centre. Chief Chundu's[1] people would travel here by canoe from the Chewore mouth to pay their taxes.

1. **Chief Chund**u — Direct descendent of Chief Chimombe, the iron god. Today Chundu's people live in the Mukwichi Tribal Lands in the Urungwe area of the Zambezi escarpment.

71

You see, the sun sinks into the mud where the river begins, far over there. All night it is washed by the water as it is carried downstream. In the morning it rises bright and clean where the Zambezi meets the sea.

The two-toed tribe

We woke up to the cries of fish eagles, mingled incongruously with the crowing of cockerels. The tsetse allows no livestock to live there apart from a few chickens. It is a tough existence, the few crops that are grown can be devastated by elephant and hippo or washed away by flood. Chief Chapota's people live on the Mwanzamtanda, a small tributary just above Kanyemba, and we had heard that there was a member of the Va-doma, the legendary two-toed tribe, living there.

We found the Va-doma's hut. It was poorly constructed and was virtually empty. Some half-naked children appeared from nowhere. The Va-doma himself had gone to collect worms for fishing so we set off towards the river. Our guide suddenly stopped and pointed at a strange footprint in the sand. The two-toed man! Someone must have been sent to call him, for a slim figure came slowly towards us, followed by a second. The two brothers stopped, staring at the camera with doleful eyes. We greeted them, trying not to stare at their extraordinary feet.

The younger man's were only marginally deformed, but the other's were like those of an ostrich. The back of the foot was normal, but the big toe was about 15 centimetres long, and the small one about six, at right angles to the first, with a cleft in between.

'In my great-great grandfather's time there were many like us. But today, we are the only two. Our children all have feet like yours,' the older one explained.

The fable that the feet have developed to enable them to climb trees to collect honey and get around easily through the rough Chewore terrain are unfounded. The deformity is a disadvantage: walking is slow and running virtually impossible.

As the moon rose like a giant yellow lantern on the horizon, we sat watching the fire flicker in the darkness. Above us the canopy of stars brought to mind a Korekore belief that the stars are candles, carried by the good spirits, *mudzimu*, so they can see in the dark. The evil spirits, *mashavi*, have no candles. Shooting stars, they say, are good spirits killing evil ones.

The Zambezi flows on into Mozambique, where it seems the good spirits and the river gods have lost control.

Larry Norton

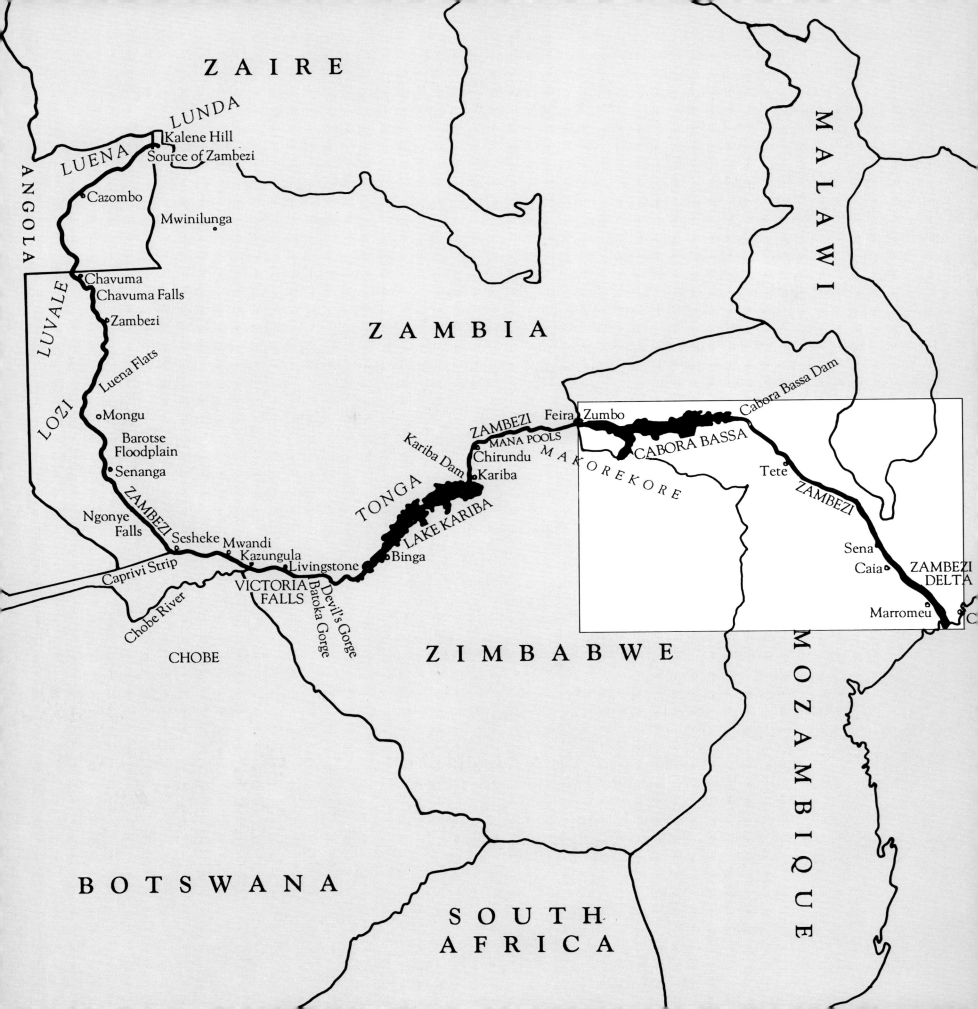

LOWER ZAMBEZI

The Portuguese technician explained, 'If we replace a pylon, "poof!" ze bandidos blow it up.'

We were sitting in a dingy cantina in the village of Songo in Mozambique, built during the construction of Cabora Bassa dam.

'What do you do?'

'Not'ing. My job is repair ze turbine when zay stop to work, but zay not work since 14 year anyway. So I do not'ing.' He laughed delightedly. It seemed incredible that an immense hydro-electric scheme had been reduced to this sorry condition.

We climbed one of the hills overlooking the wall, the only viewpoint from which we could shoot a picture without attracting attention. Sitting on a rock promontory we caught our breath and gazed down into the Kebrabassa Gorge, the great barrier against all attempts to open up the Zambezi as a trade route to the interior.

The Portuguese

Vasco da Gama, after his visit to the mouth of the Zambezi in 1498, reported to Lisbon that there were vast gold and silver reserves in the kingdom of Chief Monomatapa in Mashonaland, which could be reached by navigating the Zambezi. The idea of an African eldorado fired the Portuguese imagination. They began to set up trading posts along the coast. In 1570 an expedition was mounted in the guise of a Christian crusade under Francisco Barretto, the former Viceroy of India. 'In the opinion of many', wrote Father Monclaro, the expedition scribe and Barretto's confessor and advisor, 'it was the most brilliant company ever to set forth from Lisbon.'

The expedition sailed up the Zambezi in December 1571, unaware of their real enemies, the mosquito and tsetse fly. Men died of malaria at the rate of two or three a day. Oxen and horses collapsed from sleeping sickness. Barretto died on 25th May 1573, and the remainder of the expedition were later slaughtered by cannibals of the Zimba tribe living on the north bank of the river.

Portuguese enthusiasm for the colonization of Mozambique waned rapidly after this disaster. The floor was left open for individual Portuguese desperados and fortune-seekers to capitalize on the situation.

A state of anarchy prevailed for the next three centuries. Portuguese robber barons and their half-caste offspring set up private armies and mini kingdoms along the river, with slavery as the major economic activity. By the mid-19th century more than 15,000 slaves were sold annually through the port of Quelimane.

Into this dark scene, in 1858, came Livingstone, preparing to open up the Zambezi as 'God's highway' to the interior. His expedition up the river was soon frustrated by the impassable Kebrabassa rapids, which he had avoided on his journey two years previously.

Although Livingstone's expedition failed in its objective, it paved the way for Britain's colonial expansion into the region. Lisbon was pressurized either to put an end to the slave trade or forgo her now tenuous interests in Mozambique. In an effort to regain some control, Portugal bolstered her military forces on the Zambezi and eventually managed to overcome the robber barons. Four companies were floated, two of which were based in the Zambezi Valley with charters for the administration and development of the region.

During the first few decades of the 20th century there was more development along the Zambezi than at any time in its history. The river companies began to produce sugar as the main crop, along with coconuts, cotton, rubber, rice, groundnuts, sesame, millet and wax. By 1911 they were refining around 20,000 tonnes of sugar per year, from factories in Marromeu, Mopeia and Sena. More than three million sisal plants, and an almost equal number of coconut trees, were grown in the Quelimane district. By 1927 the Sena sugar estates comprised one of the largest sugar-growing areas in the world, producing more than 30,000 tonnes annually.

In 1928 Antonio Salazar took power in Lisbon, adopting a ferocious 'hands on' policy towards Mozambique. Its labour and natural resources were to be exploited for the sole benefit of metropolitan Portugal. Salazar imposed a restrictive foreign investment code, ensuring that Mozambique remained entirely dependent upon the mother country.

African unrest gradually increased. Frelimo (Front for the Liberation of Mozambique) was formed in June 1962. By September 1964 a guerilla war had begun in the north of the country. The following year, Ian Smith in neighbouring Rhodesia declared unilateral independence from Britain (UDI) with the object of entrenching white rule. Guerilla activities began there, leading eventually to a full-scale civil war. South Africa backed both the Portuguese and Smith regimes as they struggled to contain black nationalism.

'The big solution for the security and progress of the overseas territories,' announced the Portuguese Chief of Staff in July 1970, 'is to settle there one million whites.'

Large numbers of European immigrants were to be given farms along the Zambezi, where they would form a buffer zone to prevent Frelimo from encroaching further south. The farms would be irrigated and supplied with power from a new dam to be built in the Cabora Bassa Gorge.

The Cabora Bassa Dam

Tenders were sought for the building of the dam. A company, ZAMCO, was formed, backed financially mainly by South Africa and Portugal, with additional funding from West Germany, France, Britain and Canada. The dam was to be constructed 37 kilometres downstream from the mouth of the gorge, with an installed capacity of 3870 megawatts, as opposed to Kariba's 1200. The Luangwa, Kafue and several other tributaries enter the main river below Kariba and these, combined with the extra height of the Cabora Bassa wall, create a potential energy supply greater than that of Kariba and Aswan, on the River Nile, put together.

Work began in January 1970. The river was diverted 400 metres through underground galleries. Huge surge chambers were excavated, the largest of which is more than twice the size of St Paul's cathedral. By 5th December 1974 the project was completed. But unfortunately for the South African and Portuguese investors, a Marxist government had just taken power in Mozambique.

Political disruption

By 1973 Frelimo were in control of large areas of the country and the Portuguese were weary of war. Over the previous ten years more than 110,000 conscripts had failed to report for duty and most considered the war futile. On 25th April 1974 a military coup in Portugal ended the dictatorship there and Frelimo intensified its efforts in Mozambique. Portuguese soldiers mutinied and officers declared unofficial cease-fires throughout the country. Eventually, in September 1974, a complete handover of power to Marxist Frelimo took place and the Portuguese fled.

Rhodesian military leaders watched these events with concern. The Smith government was still firmly in the seat of power and claiming that it would remain there for the next thousand years. But their new Marxist neighbour was now willing to harbour and set up training camps for Rhodesian nationalist guerillas. To protect themselves from this event it was decided that the fostering of some kind of counter-revolution would, even if it were unable to overthrow the government, at least ensure that Mozambique remained weak and unstable.

This came in the form of the Mozambique National Resistance (MNR) which was formed by Ken Flower, then head of the Rhodesian Central Intelligence Organization (CIO). Disaffected Mozambicans would operate in their own country as *flechas* or pseudo-terrorists. Training under the CIO began on a tobacco farm in eastern Rhodesia in 1976, and so this controversial movement was born.

'The surprising ease with which the MNR developed', wrote Flower in a secret memo, 'indicated that we were proceeding along the right lines, particularly as we kept the movement small and clandestinely manageable during the first five years whilst it could provide the eyes and ears of our intelligence in Mozambique.'

A taste for brutality, once acquired, dies hard and the atrocities committed by the MNR against their own people are horrifying. The futility of the movement is illustrated by the words of an Irish missionary priest we met on our travels on the lower Zambezi:

'The MNR have no political base. They're simply gangs of murderers, looting and killing at will throughout the countryside. Sometimes rival gangs attack each other. They have no popular support and new members either have a natural inclination towards violence or they are press-ganged — young men may be forced to kill their parents or other close relatives, after which it's impossible for them to return to a normal life.'

When Zimbabwe became independent in 1980, all links with the MNR were severed and the movement was passed to South African control. The latter signed a mutual non-aggression treaty with Mozambique in 1984, the Nkomati Accord, but still terrorism beleaguers the country and the rebels continue to receive support from reactionary individuals around the world. A senior American diplomat has called it 'one of the most brutal holocausts against civilians since the Second World War'.

The ecological consequences

In retrospect the political and economic reasoning behind the construction of the Cabora Bassa Dam and the plans for Portuguese settlement seem naive and impractical. Little thought was given to the effects of the hydro-electric scheme on the downstream environment or on the people who lived there.

The wall was scheduled to close in June 1974, but was delayed for a further five months. Engineers had planned to reduce the water flow from an average of 3000 cubic metres per second to 60 for a period of four months. Ecologists had recommended that the flow be reduced to 400 – 500 cubic metres per second, which meant that the lake would take about 18 months to fill. Instead, in a bid to make up time, the Portuguese decided to cut down the water flow to 60 cubic metres *per day*.

December through February should have been the spawning season for the river's fish, but they were not left with sufficient water below the dam wall in which to survive, let alone breed. Hundreds of thousands were stranded, rotting on the banks. Lake Danga on the floodplain dried up completely, destroying the livelihood of its African fishermen. Compensation was never considered and no voices were raised on their behalf. Citizens' lobbies to prevent this sort of occurrence do not exist in primitive Africa.

Nor could they rely upon their crops to make up the protein deficit. Annual floods had always washed away the excessive salinity of the soil, and without them it became impossible to produce the traditional foods. This might well have happened anyway, but so inadequate had the environmental impact study been that nobody foresaw the crisis. Ancient hardwood forests were razed and given to contractors to dispose of as they would. No replanting was done.

Ecologists Tinman and Souza Dias drew up proposals for an Operation-Noah-style rescue of the large mammals. They planned to set up a base camp between Bangwe mountain on the south bank and the Dague river, about 30 kilometres west of Chicoa. Black rhino, roan antelope, tsessebe and cheetah were to be captured and moved to a new game reserve planned in the vicinity of the camp. All other species would be herded by helicopters to the mainland. The Galomagapfhue Plain, south of the Mague hills and about half way down the lake, was also to be registered as a National Park. But nothing came of the plans — the Portuguese government concluded that it would be too expensive.

In 1990 the water flow is normal again but the fauna of the lower Zambezi may never recover. Even the Zambezi shark *(Carcharhinus leucas)*, which used to swim upriver from the sea, is now seldom seen. Before Cabora Bassa was built the shark was found as far up as the Kariba gorge. It is notorious as a man-eater in east African waters and at least 90 percent of the shark attacks off the Mozambique coast have been caused by this species.

It has been known to attack hippos and was probably responsible for several of the human fatalities attributed to crocodiles. Perhaps the local people should thank the Caborra Bassa team for ridding them of one menace — certainly they have no other reason to express gratitude. In the words of ecologist Dr Bryan Davies, the dam was a 'smash and grab raid on the natural resources of this poor country.'

Entry into Mozambique

The Zambezi enters Mozambique at the top end of Lake Cabora Bassa, where it is joined by the Luangwa, a tributary nearly a quarter its size. On the north bank squats a scruffy line of tin huts with an empty cantina at one end. This is Zumbo, founded by the Portuguese in the early 17th century as a trading fair. Selous comments that nearly 200 years before his visit in 1882 it had been a flourishing place, with a governor, a Catholic church and a college, trading in ivory and gold dust. By the time he passed through there were only five resident Portuguese, whom he described as 'mere wrecks of men, frail, yellow and fever-stricken.' Zumbo has never regained its former prosperity.

The man-made lake of Cabora Bassa is long and deep, with heavily forested islands and is surrounded by rugged hills. There are about 20 permanent islands formed from the Gamwenje hills near the Messenguezi / Zambezi confluence, which cover roughly 25 square kilometres. Apart from these and Manherere, a large island situated opposite Bangue mountain, most of the others are tiny islets. The lake shore is becoming choked with water hyacinth (*Eichkornia crassipes*), which floats down from the area below Kariba and forms large mats in the quiet backwaters. There is no mechanism for dealing with it, so the plant will either spread, unchecked, or gradually vanish of its own accord.

A concession has been made to a Zimbabwean hunter to kill crocodiles in the lake; another has been granted for the slaughter of hippos. It seems unlikely that any of the remaining wildlife along the lakeshore will be salvaged without a formal conservation policy.

Tete

As the river emerges from the gorge below the dam and lake, it gradually widens between rocky banks. Denuded of large trees and singularly lacking in bird and animal life, there is little to catch the eye until one reaches the town of Tete, which was established in 1531 as an advance post of the intended gold trade with the Mwene Mtapa.

Piles of rubbish surround the crumbling walls and bare, smashed windows of the once quaint little Portuguese houses. *Viva la guerra popular*, proclaims a torn and yellowed poster.

In the dusty street by the river stands the red-roofed cathedral, its bell hanging green and cobwebbed, ropeless. The old teak door has been torn from its hinges and the pews ripped from the concrete floor. A portrait of Lenin, scratched in charcoal, adorns the vestry in place of the Blessed Virgin, and behind the altar a hard-eyed soldier is depicted holding, at bayonet point, a man clutching a money bag. Outside in the street pot-bellied children stretch out their hands, their eyes pleading. Flies crawl into their nostrils and ears. A woman, wracked with malaria, lies moaning in the gutter.

Tete is a town of refugees, soldiers and aid workers. The elderly are conspicuous by their absence. Mankind's allotted three score and ten has somehow eluded the inhabitants of this unhappy place. The surrounding woodland has disappeared in a widening dustbowl. Peasants scratch among the rocks with their hoes and watch their crops wither and die. Wind and rain have eroded the topsoil and formed deep gullies, which become swamps during the rains, a quagmire of human misery. A daily convoy of trucks, loaded with goods destined for Malawi, rumbles across the suspension bridge over the Zambezi.

On course for the sea

A little polluted by the experience of Tete the Zambezi flows on towards the sea, widening from 500 metres wide to two kilometres, the monotony eased by the occasional rocky outcrop. Animal life on the lower Zambezi is a grave disappointment: not a single hippopotamus, crocodile or antelope is to be seen, except in the delta. Even the bird life is poor, due partially to the decimation of the fish population by the Cabora Bassa project. The large animals were eliminated mainly in the latter half of the 19th century and any remaining wildlife is now being hunted to extinction by the MNR.

Seventy kilometres below Tete the river passes through the Lupata gorge, where sheer cliffs of alkaline and rayolite rise 100 metres above the water. Below Lupata the now sluggish Zambezi prepares itself for the sea and a maze of channels, islands and reed banks spreads five to eight kilometres wide. Now and then patches of forest grasp the banks, but most of these have been cut for dug-out canoes or as fuel for the paddle steamers which used to ply the river in the first few decades of this century. The riverine peoples have little tribal identity. By 1880 the Ngungwes, from the Tete area, and the Senas, from further down the river, had been caught up in the maelstrom of the slave trade and mixed together. Most below the Lupata gorge call themselves Senas, although Sena is no longer a tribe but rather a small town where a railway bridge crosses the Zambezi, linking Mozambique with Malawi to the north. Today it is occupied by bandits and the railway is no more than two lines of overgrown rust and a dangerously neglected bridge.

Bandit country

Since we would be unlikely to survive the journey through rebel country by canoe or motor dinghy, we took to the air and flew in a Cessna 206, often only 15 metres above the water. Our intrepid pilot was Richard Calder. We landed at Marromeu, about 100 kilometres from the river mouth. A group of camouflaged figures surrounded the aircraft. Trying to appear casual, we swung open the door and clambered onto the wing. Pilot Calder turned on his winning smile.

'Bon die! Constat!' they shouted in unison.

It was okay; they were friendly. We were escorted through the streets of Marromeu, which had once been a thriving centre of the sugar trade. Bandits, we were told, had recently occupied the town for 16 days. Every wall and signpost was riddled with bullet holes and we wondered how they managed to obtain enough ammunition for such profligate wastage. They had raked the entire settlement with automatic fire like children with a garden hose. We passed the Banquo de Marromeu, its crumbling walls overgrown with creepers and one side blown out by a bomb.

'Bandidos,' explained one of the soldiers, 'they try to rob bank, but find nothing. No money in Mozambique.' He laughed uproariously at his own joke.

A woman was crouched under a lamp-post. Two naked babies, pitifully thin, competed for her milk and she looked at us sadly. As we were giving her a packet of dried apricots, a legless man swung past on his fists. Across the road a paunchy army commander bellowed at some children who were walking too close to his headquarters.

Every week a Red Cross aircraft drops supplies for the villagers as part of an ongoing aid programme and a DAK flew in the next day — piloted, ironically, by a South African from Pretoria. He was closely followed by a couple of Soviet MIL 8 helicopters, which came to resupply the Frelimo soldiers. Neither wasted any time in leaving.

The factory dominated the skyline. Railway locomotives in pristine condition stood in the siding, their wheels overgrown with weeds. Caterpillars, tractors, front-end loaders, Landrovers and cranes stood in neat rows, abandoned. Tons of sophisticated machinery remained intact within the building. Factories in the Ruhr Valley must have looked like this in 1945, while Germany waited helplessly for the allied forces to close in. The Portuguese, it seemed, had simply switched out the lights and left.

The Zambezi Delta

We had read that vast herds of buffalo lived in the Zambezi Delta, and elephants with pink legs, which had lost the skin pigment from standing all their lives in the swamps. We doubted that much game had survived, but we were assured that there were still plenty of buffalo in the delta.

The Zambezi Delta is a triangle of 18,000 square kilometres, with a sea frontage of 120 kilometres, much of which is now savanna grassland because the dam has reduced the amount of flooding. Tinman reports that there were at least 130,000 buffalo in the delta at one time. Most of them were shot during the Second World War; whole herds wantonly massacred, sometimes for meat, sometimes purely for sport, like the bison on the prairies of North America. Large numbers of elephant, hippo, zebra and waterbuck roamed the plains and swamps. The last of the elephants with large tusks were shot from helicopters during an oil exploration of the delta.

We decided to fly up the Zambezi as far as the Shire confluence and then use our second fuel tank to search the delta. The river coiled brown and sluggish beneath our wheels as we buzzed over the water at treetop height. On the south bank the remains of

Shupanga, now called Lacedonia, could be seen with its little church where Mary Livingstone lies buried, her grave neglected and overgrown. Bandits have ravaged the church and the surrounding buildings are roofless and pock-marked. Presently Mount Morrumbala loomed out of the plain, rising over 1000 metres above sea level, a beacon and guide to dozens of early explorers of the Zambezi.

End of a journey

Turning back at the Shire confluence we flew inland over old forests and abandoned plantations of coconut trees. The forests gave way to an open, swampy plain, stretching unbroken to the horizon. This was buffalo country. We saw them quite suddenly, tiny black dots on the green. Richard dropped the revs and roared in low. A herd of 300 or 400 strong turned together and began to gallop across the plain, flocks of egrets whirling around their dark bodies. We found a dozen herds without deviating from our course, varying in numbers between 20 and 400 animals. Waterbuck shared the grazing, sometimes with the buffalo and sometimes in pockets of their own. We saw no elephant or hippopotamus but at least there was a breeding nucleus of buffalo from which the herds could one day regain their former strength. Buffalo, when unmolested, breed with extraordinary rapidity, as do elephant, providing there are enough mature bulls to service the cow herds.

Our tanks were low now and we flew down the main river channel towards the coast. At the mouth lay the wreck of a Portuguese freighter, dark and ugly on the clean sand. Other wrecks have lain there over the centuries. The dreams of an African eldorado, which inspired an expedition of 'the most brilliant company ever to set forth from Lisbon', were shattered forever by this treacherous waterway. And for Livingstone, two centuries later, this spot must surely have signified for him the bitter knowledge that the Zambezi was not after all to be God's highway to the interior.

Although much of Mozambique is a shocking testimony to thoughtless greed and destruction, our journey through the middle, and even upper Zambezi, has served as a stark reminder of the necessity of preserving what is left of this precious wilderness and its rare abundance of wildlife. A wave of conservation has brought the elephants into the limelight. As they rumble their infrasonic messages across the bush, their future is being decided at conference tables on the other side of the world. We hope their fate is not just a guise for political lobbying and that the decisions made will be to their advantage. People everywhere are beginning to fight against the decimation of their natural heritage, aware that man himself will be the ultimate victim. Can any responsible government afford to ignore this surge of protest?

COLOUR PLATES

1. On a signal from the matriarch, a herd of elephants head back to the security of denser vegetation at dawn. Elephants have a complex communication system, much of it transmitted below the range of human hearing. The infrasonic signals are heard and interpreted by other elephants, often many kilometres away.

2. The source of the Zambezi, just a few kilometres from that of the Congo.

3. Morning dew clings to the web of a golden orb spider (Nephila family).

4. A golden orb spider consumes its freshly caught prey.

Mating net-winged beetles (Lycidae family)

5. An *arum frog* (Hyperolius horskokii) *nestles in the folds of an arum lily.*

6. *We camped on the river, swimming and bathing in the cold, gurgling pools, fringed by dense woodland. It is a lepidopterist's and herpetologist's paradise.*

7. *Moonrise. 40 kilometres from its source the river cascades over a granite batholith on its westward course. Nearby caves were used as collection points for the slave gangs before their long march to the sea.*

8. *Young Angolans fishing in the river about 80 kilometres from the source.*

9. *Lunda boys swim in the Zambezi near its source.*

10. *An Angolan girl fords the river.*

10

11. *Fishing nets dry in the morning sun near Chitokiloki mission.*

12. *A lone figure strides across a beach below Chavuma.*

13. *The turbulence of the water has created a deep basin below the Chavuma rapids. A wooden dug-out plies back and forward, carrying people, goats, bicycles and almost every other commodity from one bank to the other.*

11

12

Malachite kingfisher
(Alcedo cristata)

14. *The Kashiji river, a tributary of the Zambezi.*

15. *Sundown over the Barotse floodplain.*

16. *A Lozi fisherman paddles his dug-out on the Barotse floodplain.*

16

17. *Water lilies*
(Nymphaea petersiana) *form an underwater garden in the Barotse floodplain.*

18. *The bird life is abundant and accustomed to boats. A goliath heron (*Ardea goliath) *takes off in the dusk.*

19 and 20. *The Kuomboka Ceremony. The barge and the bodyguard await the king's imminent arrival at the annual ritual celebrating the flooding of the Barotse floodplain.*

21. *The king (nalikwanda) of the Lozi tribe is transported by barge down the river.*

22. *The king's bodyguard leads the procession. These paddlers wear a crown of bird feathers, mishukwe, on their heads.*

23. *The barge paddlers wear the traditional* siziba, *an animal-skin skirt. They place a red beret bearing an insert of lion's mane on their heads.*

24. *The horse shoe shaped Ngonye Falls.*

25. *Outside the villages near Senanga, the day's catch is hung on stakes. Fresh tigerfish and bream shine in the sun tempting the passing traveller.*

26. *A lone tree looms over the Chobe swamps.*

27. *The river near Katimo Mulilo, which means 'quenching fires'. The town acquired its name from the rapids by which it is situated. For in the days before flints and matches the natives carried a fire in their dug-outs so they could cook as they travelled upstream. But on reaching the rapids here the water would invariably wash over the bows and douse the flames.*

28. *An African spoonbill* (Platalea alba) *sweeps for food on a Chobe pan. The odd-shaped bill is an adaptation for catching small fish and aquatic invertebrates.*

29. *A vervet monkey* (Cercopithecus aethiops) *plays among devilthorn flowers near the Chobe Zambezi confluence.*

30. *A black-winged stilt* (Himantopus himantopus) *wades delicately through the shallows.*

31. *A summer sky outlines the silhouette of an approaching elephant near the Chobe river.*

32. *A female fish eagle (Haliaeetus vocifer), larger and heavier than her mate, prepares to consume a fish which she has just pirated from him.*

33. *A thorn bush in stark relief against the sky.*

34. *A frankolin keeps a lonely vigil on a termite mound.*

35. *Evening sky during the rains.*

36

37

36. *A bat-eared fox (Otocyon megalotis) approaches its daytime refuge. The huge ears are adapted for listening to the movements of subterranean insect life.*

37. *A dung beetle struggles to roll his nuptial ball as the female inspects his handiwork. The dung is used to feed the white grub-like larvae.*

38. *An elephant herd enjoy an evening dustbath.*

38

39

39. *A leopard returning to the forest after an evening drink in the Chobe. The pattern of the coat provides a perfect camouflage in the dappled light of the forest.*

40

40. Hippos may attack a canoe if they are prevented from reaching the safety of a deep-water channel.

41. Elephants mud-bathing at a Chobe pan. Social interaction between individuals is important in the highly complex society of these mammals.

42. A yellow-billed stork (Mycteria ibis) snaps a small fish between its mandibles.

43. A white-headed vulture (Aegypius occipitalis) in flight. This species generally seems to be one of the first at kills. We have often found leopard kills by observing the behaviour of these birds.

44. *A Tonga fish trap near Katombora.*

45. *Elephants at water in the tranquility of a Chobe evening.*

46. *A cricket consumes leaf litter near the Chobe.*

47. *A velvet mite (Acarina) emerges with the first rains.*

48. *A Swainson's frankolin strides jauntily past our hide.*

49. *Spotted hyenas (Crocuta crocuta) mill around the carcass of a kudu they have killed themselves. Contrary to popular belief, hyenas are not merely scavengers, but are often active predators.*

50. *A kudu bull peers through the undergrowth. Kudu are ruminating browsers and will eat grass only in exceptional circumstances.*

51. 'Scenes such as these
must have been gazed
upon by angels in their
flight' wrote Livingstone
of the river above the
falls. A pair of Egyptian
geese (Alpochen
aegyptiacus) stand
almost on the brink of the
Devil's Cataract.

52. A view from Devil's
Cataract.

53. The Victoria Falls.
The Devil's Cataract by
night.

54. Cecil Rhodes insisted
that the bridge be built
just below the Falls so
that the spray would soak
the railway carriages.

55. Fungi grow easily in
the perpetual damp of the
rain forest.

56. A mass of bloodlilies
(Haemanthus
multiflorus) adorn the
rain forest in November.

57. A bolt of lightning
lights up the night sky.

55

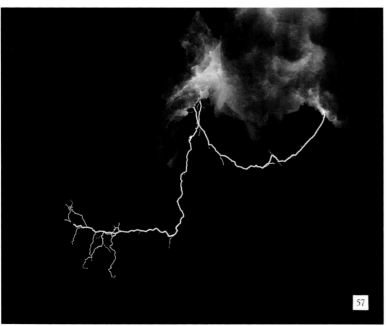

57

56

58. *A foaming wall of water pounds over the dark basalt cliff of the Main Falls.*

59. *A bushbuck (Tragelaphus scriptus) in the rain forest. These are shy creatures, best observed in the early morning, at the peak of their feeding activity.*

60. *When crocodile hatchlings break out of their shells and start squeaking, the female will gather them gently in her mouth and transport them to the water's edge.*

61. *A vervet monkey with her young in the rain forest. In this case it is the mother's own baby, but monkey females will happily accept a strange infant, vying for an opportunity to become a foster mother.*

62

62. *An orphaned vervet monkey clings to its 'foster mother', a Tonga headman.*

63. *Life is hard for the Tonga, one of Africa's most primitive tribes.*

64. *Dysabello, the old Tonga story teller.*

63

65. The Tonga live in a world of dreams, of long-dead ancestors in baobab trees, of rainmakers and river gods, and witches straddling the backs of hyenas.

66. There seems little need for clothing in the lives of these people.

67. Cheerful in spite of his handicap, a young Tonga boy carries his dogs and fishing nets to the river.

68. The headman's wife at a Tonga funeral, Sinazongwe. The Tonga have a strong belief in the after-life and take great care of their dead.

69. The old women smoke hubble bubble pipes made from gourds filled with dagga (Cannabis sativa) and wear sticks through holes in their noses, formed in their youth from piercing the nostrils with a thorn. Toothless gums attest to the Kulangwa ceremony, in which the four front teeth were knocked out to enhance the beauty of teenage girls.

70. A Tonga bride and her handmaiden. In preparation for the wedding the bride is kept in a hut for a few days to make her skin paler.

127

71 and 72. *Tonga women scoop kapenta off the drying racks.*

73. *Kapenta are caught with huge round gill nets lowered from pontoons into the water.*

74. *Lake Kariba.*

75. *A bolt of lightning explodes into a Matusadona hillside.*

76. *A haunting shoreline in Matusadona National Park.*

77. *Moonrise over Matusadona.*

78. *A young fish eagle stretches its wings in preparation for its maiden flight. It is now about 60 days old.*

79. *Pylons at Kariba, carrying power from the hydro-electric scheme to the capital of Zimbabwe.*

80. *The lake has actually enhanced rather than detracted from the natural beauty of the area.*

81. *Changing the guard; goliath herons exchange incubation duties. The pale greenish-blue eggs take about four weeks to hatch.*

82. *Although the lake is the centre of much tourist activity, it has still retained a beauty and tranquillity typical of Africa.*

83. *The Kariba Gorge.*

84. *A cardinal woodpecker feeds its young.*

85. *Young green-backed herons* (Butorides striatus) *imitating reeds to deceive the 'predator'. This characteristic 'bittern posture' is used by many herons as a form of self-defence.*

86. *A black-headed heron* (Ardea melanocephala) *feeding in the Kariba shallows. Herons may stand motionless for long spells waiting for a fish to swim within reach.*

86

87. *A baobab (Adansonia digitata) presides over the Zambezi Valley during the rains. Recent carbon-dating techniques have shown that some of these great trees are up to 3000 years old.*

88. *Grey-headed gulls (Larus cirrocephalus) stand on top of a termite mound on an island in Kariba. Breeding colonies may number many hundreds of birds.*

89. *A reed cormorant (Phalacrocorax africanus) catching the last light of the day in a characteristic pose, as it dries its wings.*

90. *An African skimmer (Rhynchops flavirostris) cuts the water with its lower mandible as it skims for fish. A reflex action of the bill snaps it shut as it comes in contact with its prey.*

90

92

94. Impala does at water. If one sits quietly in a hide, impala will often walk within a couple of metres of it, unaware of human presence.

91. 'As fine a picture as I have ever seen in Africa', wrote Livingstone of this area in 1856.

92. The lonely footprints of a marabou stork (Leptoptilos crumeniferus) cross the sand in Mana Pools.

93. Acacia albida trees form a cathedral in the late afternoon sun at Mana Pools.

94. Impala does at water. If one sits quietly in a hide, impala will often walk within a couple of metres of it, unaware of human presence.

95. Dwarf mongooses (Helogale parvula) surveying the terrain for signs of danger. They are brave little animals, readily attacking snakes and other poisionous creatures. When catching a large snake the whole troop may take part, encircling the reptile and taking turns to dash in and administer a bite before springing out of harm's way.

96. A cheetah drags its freshly killed prey, an impala doe, into thicker cover. It will then utter a strange chirp to call its companions to the carcass.

97

97. *Baboons live in troops of up to 50 individuals and maintain a rigid hierarchy.*

98. *A landscape at Mana Pools. Saddlebill storks* (Ephippiorhynchus senegalensis) *share a pan with an elephant.*

99. *Zebras at water in a parched landscape.*

100. *Carmine bee-eaters*
(Merops nubicoides)
outside their nest holes.
They start breeding in
huge colonies in the banks
of the Zambezi in
September.

100

101, 102 and 103.
*Lions mating. The female
initiates the act, which
takes only a few seconds,
but may be repeated
every 15 minutes or so
for several days.*

104. *An elephant bull uses a termite mound as a step while stretching for the branch of an Acacia albida tree.*

105. *A view of the Zambezi at Mana Pools.*

106. *A rhinoceros charge.*

107. *Helmeted guineafowl* (Numida meleagris) *scratch in the dust at dawn. They are highly gregarious except when breeding.*

108. *Courtney Selous described them as the most common of the big mammals but today, only 100 years later, the black rhinoceros* (Diceros biconis) *is facing extinction. In 1960 there were estimated to be one million black rhinos in Africa. By 1980 approximately 15,000 remained, and today there are probably less than 3500.*

109. *A hippo emerges from shallow water where it wallows for most of the day to keep its skin moist.*

109

110. A baboon crosses a flooded creek, showing his distaste for the water.

111. African skimmers.

112. A flock of redbilled quelea taking off. Individual colonies may number several million birds.

113. A crocodile female protecting her eggs.

110

111

White-fronted bee-eater (Merops bullockiodes)

114. *Mating leopards have rarely been observed in the wild.*

115. *Impala have scent glands on their fetlocks. Jumping and kicking their legs in the presence of danger may disperse a warning smell to others in the herd.*

116

117

116. *As we canoe past him, an elephant shows his displeasure at our presence.*

117. *A dwarf mongoose peers inquisitively from its refuge in a mopane tree.*

118. *A leopard drags its prize, an impala ram, to the safety of a Natal mahogany (Trichilia emetica). They often lodge their prey in the fork of a tree to keep it away from lions and hyenas, either of which may force the leopard off its kill.*

119. *A spotted hyena approaches the remains of a leopard kill, in this case a young impala ram.*

120. *A pied kingfisher hovers over the water before arrowing down on its prey.*

121. *A bloated lion cub by the remains of a buffalo. A hooded vulture awaits its turn.*

122. *Impala rams with their horns locked in combat.*

123. *A buffalo bull with red-billed oxpeckers* (Buphagus erythrorhynchus) *in attendance. Lone bulls can be extremely dangerous.*

124. A grey heron with a catfish. The catches of herons are often pirated by fish eagles before they have a chance to eat them.

125. A hammerkop (Scopus umbretta) dives for a frog. The bird is regarded as an evil omen in African folklore and huts may be burned after a hammerkop has passed overhead.

126. A saddlebilled stork fishing on a pan.

127. Standing tall with ears outstretched, an elephant bull threatens the photographer, but will rarely charge.

128

128. A leopard descends gracefully from its resting place in an Acacia albida tree.

129. Baboons are acutely observant; attempting to hide from them is a futile effort and it is best to show oneself and let them gradually relax in one's presence.

130. A herd of buffalo stampedes up a bank.

129

163

131. A (Cassine schlechterana) *tree robed in the ghostly web of a caterpillar which feeds on the leaves and pupates into a small grey moth within the web.*

132. *Elephants have reduced this baobab tree to a mass of pulp. The elephants will eat most of it and the remains will probably be infected by a virus to which baobabs are vulnerable when so exposed. Eventually no trace of the tree will remain.*

133. *The kudu is both wary and fleet of foot. Here a cow searches carefully for signs of danger before drinking at a waterhole.*

164

134. *Zebra and impala share a waterhole, always nervously on the lookout for predators.*

135. *The fish eagle can see a fish near the surface from a distance of several hundred metres. Here a female swoops in to seize its prey.*

136. *Elephants at water.*

137. *Elephant calves often take up aggressive postures, but will quickly run back to their mothers if the 'enemy' shows no sign of retreating.*

138. *A hammerkop lunges for a frog.*

139. *A bushfire in Zambia, which will rage for months, burning thousands of square kilometres of veld before it eventually peters out. The fires are lit deliberately by Zambians seeking to catch animals trapped by the flames.*

140. 'A long time ago a woman had a child with feet 'zvigunwe zviri' (two-toed), like mine. She had eaten animals with two feet which she had caught in the hills while she was pregnant. The tribe killed the child. The next child was just the same and they killed him too. When the third child was born with the strange feet, they said the spirits had willed it, and they let him live. Since then many of us have had two toes, but only the men.'

141. His walk is a rolling gait on the triangular shaped base of his foot, one foot being placed in front of the other to enable him to balance. The deformity is actually transmitted by an autosomal dominant, semi-penetrant gene, hence the variations in the degree of abnormality.

142. A flash flood of a small tributary nearly leaves us stranded.

143. Wind erosion forms delicate patterns in the sand of the river banks.

144. The Iron God. The Makorekore tribe believes it to be the embodiment of Chief Chimombe of the Va-Sori tribe.

145. The remote, inaccessible Mupata Gorge, home to a huge variety of wildlife.

146. *Cabora Bassa wall.*
Kebrabassa means 'the
end of work'. The slaves
who rowed boats up the
river from the coast so
named the gorge and the
rapids as they could travel
no further.

147. *The upper reaches*
of Cabora Bassa with
Zumbo hill in the
background.

148. *Cabora Bassa after*
a flood down the Zambezi
and Luangwa rivers.

149. *The turbines in the*
Cabora Bassa wall have
not been properly
operational for 15 years.
In 1989 the hydro-
electric scheme was
operating at 0.02 percent
of its capacity.

150. *Tete is a town of refugees, soldiers and aid workers.*

151. *Once intended as an advance post for the prosperous trade of gold, the town of Tete is now a shadow of its former self.*

152. *Peasants living near Tete scratch among the rocks with their hoes and watch their crops wither and die.*

152

153. *The deserted factory dominates the skyline at Marromeu.*

154. *Soviet helicopters fly into Marromeu at regular intervals to drop supplies for the Frelimo soldiers.*

155. *Friend or foe? A Frelimo soldier in Marromeu.*

155

156

156. A fisherman on the Zambezi Delta, his catches greatly diminished by the construction of the Cabora Bassa Dam upstream.

157. Buffalo thrive in herds of 300 or 400 on the open grassy plains of the Zambezi Delta.

158. The wreck of a Portuguese freighter lies stranded on the sandy stretches at the mouth of the Zambezi.

BIBLIOGRAPHY

Axelson, E (1960), *Portuguese in South East Africa 1600-1700*, Witwatersrand University Press, Johannesburg

Axelson, E (1973), *Portuguese in South East Africa 1488-1600*, C Struik, Cape Town

Balinsky, B I & James, G V (1960), Explosive reproduction of organisms in the Kariba lake, *South African Journal of Science*, vol 56, pp 101-104

Barnes, T (1858-1859), Notes on the Zambezi Expedition, *Proceedings of the Royal Geographical Society*, vol 3, pp 99-106

Bond, G (1975), The Geology and Formation of the Victoria Falls, *Mosi-oa-Tunya a handbook to the Victoria Falls*, Edited by D W Phillipson, Longman, Salisbury, Rhodesia

Boxer, C A (1960), *An African Eldorado — Monomatapa and Mozambique 1498-1752*, Historical Association of Rhodesia and Nyasaland

Bruce, N (1975), *Portugal — the last empire*, David & Charles, Newton Abbot

Clark, J D (Dec 1952), Origin and spelling of the name Zambezi, *Northern Rhodesia Journal*, no 6, pp 69-71

Clark, J D (1975), Stone Age man at the Victoria Falls, *Mosi-oa-Tunya a handbook to the Victoria Falls*, edited by D W Phillipson, Longman, Salisbury, Rhodesia

Clements, F (1959), *Kariba: the struggle with the river god*, Methuen & Co, London

Colson, E & Gluckman, M (1959), *Seven tribes of British Central Africa*, Revised ed, Manchester University Press for Rhodes Livingstone Institute

Coillard, F (1971), *On the threshold of central Africa — a record of twenty years' pioneering among the Barotsi of the upper Zambezia*, 3rd ed, Frank Cass and Co Ltd, London

Davidson, B (1979), The revolution of people's power, Notes on Mozambique, 1979, *Race and Class*, vol 21, no 2, pp 127-143

Davies, B (1975), They pulled the plug out of the lower Zambezi, *African Wildlife*, vol 29, no 2, pp 26-27.

Duffy, J (1959), *Portuguese Africa*, Harvard University Press, Cambridge, Massachusettes du Toit, R F (1982), *A preliminary assessment of the environmental implications of the proposed Mupata and Batoka hydro-electric schemes*, Natural Resources Board, Harare

du Toit, R F & Stanning J (May 1981), Investigation of likely enviromental impacts of possible projects on the Zambezi River, *Zimbabwe Science News*, vol 15, no 5, pp 115-119

Financial Gazette (23 March 1989), Worries over implications of Zambezi oil exploration, p 5

Gray, R (1971), Portuguese musketeers on the Zambezi, *Journal of African History*, vol 12, no 4, pp 531-533

Henriksen, T H (Oct 1978), Marxism and Mozambique, *African affairs*, vol 77, no 309, pp 441-462

Hughes, R S, *Chewore — history of the area*, New Paper

Hudson, R S (Jul-Dec 1935), The human geography of Balovale district, Northern Rhodesia, *Journal of the Royal Anthropological Institute of Great Britain & Ireland*, vol 65, pp 235-266

Isaacman, A F (1976), The tradition of resistance in Mozambique, *Anti-colonial activity in the Zambezi Valley 1850-1921*, Heinemann, London

Isaacman, A F (1985), Mozambique — tugging at the chains of dependency, *African crises and United States Foreign Policy*, University of California

Jackson, P & Davies, B (May 1976), Caborra Bassa in its first year — some ecological aspects and comparisons, *Rhodesia Science News*, vol 10, no 5, pp 128-133

Jaster, R S (Nov-Dec 1985), The security outlook in Mozambique, *Survival*, pp 258-264

Kenmuir, D (1978), *A wilderness called Kariba*, Wilderness Publication, Salisbury, Rhodesia

Kirk, Dr J (1965), The Zambezi Journal, *Letters of Dr John Kirk*, vols 1 and 2, ed Reginald Foskett, Oliver & Boyd, Edinburgh & London

Lamplugh, G W (1907), Geology of the Zambezi basin around Batoka Gorge, *Quarterly Journal of the Geological Society*, vol 63, pp 162-216

Lancaster, C S (1974), Ethnic identity, history and tribe in the middle Zambezi Valley, *American Ethnologist*, vol 1, no 4, pp 707-730

Livingstone, Dr D (1956), *The Zambezi expedition of David Livingstone 1858-1863*, ed J P R Wallis, Chatto & Windus Ltd, London

Livinstone, Dr D (1858), *Missionary travels and researches in South Africa*, Harper & Row, New York

Lyne, R N (1913), *Mozambique — its agricultural development*, Fisher Unwin, London

MacDonald, J F (1955), *Zambezi River*, MacMillan & Co, London

Martelli, G (1970), *Livingstone's river: a history of the Zambezi Expedition 1858-1864*, Chatto & Windus, London

Maugham, R (1910), *Zambezia — a general description of the Zambezi River from its delta to the river Aroangwa*, John Murray, London

Middlemass, K (1975), *Caborra Bassa engineering and politics in southern Africa*, Weidenfeld and Nicolson, London

Molyneux, A J (1905), The Zambezi River and the Victoria Falls, *Proceedings of the Rhodesia Scientific Association*, vol 5, pp 25-29

Molyneux, A J (1905), The physical history of the Victoria Falls, *Geographical Journal*, vol 25, pp 40-55

Mpofu, S M (Mar and Apr 1987), DDT and its use in Zimbabwe, *Zimbabwe Science News*, vol 21, nos 3 and 4, pp 31-36

Newitt, M (1973), *Portuguese settlement on the 'Zambezi; Exploration, land tenure and colonial rule in East Africa*, Longmans, London

Newitt, M (1974), Toward a history of modern Mozambique, *Rhodesian History*, vol 5, pp 33-47

Newitt, M (1981), *Portugal in Africa, the last hundred years*, Hurst, London

Oliver, H (1975), Damit, Macmillan, Johannesburg

Radmann, W (Summer 1974), The Zambezi development scheme — Caborra Bassa, *Issue*, vol 4, no 2, pp 47-54

Robins, E & Legge, R (1959), *Animal Dunkirk, The story of Lake Kariba and 'Operation Noah', the greatest animal rescue since the Ark*, Herbert Jenkins, London

Selous, F C (1889), Letters — Journey to the Kafue River and the upper Zambezi, *Proceedings of the Royal Geographical Society*, 2nd series, vol 7, pp 216-223

Selous, F C (1881), Journeys in the interior of south-central Africa, *Proceedings of the Royal Geographical Society*, 2nd series, vol 3, pp 169-175

Smith, A K (1973), The peoples of southern Mozambique, a historical survey, *Journal of African History*, vol 14, no 4, pp 565-580

Smith, A K (1974), Antonia Salazar and the reversal of Portuguese colonial policy, *Journal of African History*, vol 15, no 4, pp 653-667

Smithers, R H (April 1959), The Kariba lake, *Oryx*, vol 5, no 1, pp21-24

Steel, Maj E A (Jul-Dec 1917), Zambezi-Congo watershed, *Geographical Journal*, vol 50, pp 180-199

Syabbalo, E , *Tonga crafts in figures*, Sinazeze, Zambezi

Theal, G M (1964), *Records of south-eastern Africa*, Struik, Cape Town

Tomlinson, B N (1977), The Mozambique Company, *Journal of African History*, vol 18, no 2, pp 283-286.

Vail, L & White, L (1980), *Capitalism and colonialism in Mozambique, a study of Queliamene District*, Heinemann, London

Vail, L & White, L (Fall 1979), The struggle for Mozambique — capitalist rivalries 1900-1940, *Review*, vol 3, no 2, pp 243-288

Vail, L (1976), Mozambique's chartered companies — the rule of the feeble, *Journal of African History*, vol 17, no 3, pp 389-416

White, J D (1971), History and customs of the Urungwe district, *Nada*, vol 10, no 3, pp 33-72

Wild, H (1964), A guide to the flora of the Victoria Falls, *The Victoria Falls*, ed B M Fagan Livingstone, Zambia

Williams, E L (1974), African giant, the saga of Caborra Bassa, *Optima*, vol 24, no 3, pp95-105

INDEX

Figures in italics refer to captions